D1385475

SWANSEA LIBRARIES
6000339728

The Greatest Scarlets XV Ever

(Colorsport/Colin Elsey)

(PA Images)

The Greatest Scarlets XV Ever

Phil Bennett

To all those who have had the honour
of wearing the Scarlet jersey

Published in 2014 by
Gomer Press, Llandysul, Ceredigion, SA44 4JL

ISBN 978 1 84851 886 5

A CIP record for this title is available from the British Library

This book is published with the financial support of the Welsh Books Council

The publishers would also like to acknowledge the contributions made by the Huw Evans Picture Agency, Colorsport and the Press Association to the publication of this book.

www.huwevansimages.com

www.colorsport.co.uk

www.pressassociation.co.uk

Printed and bound in Wales at
Gomer Press, Llandysul, Ceredigion

Contents

Second-row forward (and connoisseur of outside-half play) Willie John McBride, captaining the 1974 Lions against South Africa in Port Elizabeth.

(Colorsport/Colin Elsey)

Foreword

To read *The Greatest Scarlets XV Ever* is to read the 'Who's Who' of rugby. But there is one howling error in it. One glaring omission. More of which in a minute.

Whenever I think of Llanelli R.F.C. and Stradey Park, I hear a roll call of rugby greats: Ivor Jones, Lewis Jones, Carwyn James, R.H. Williams, Delme Thomas, Derek Quinnell, J.J. Williams, Ray Gravell, Scott Quinnell, Ieuan Evans, Simon Easterby, Dwayne Peel and Stephen Jones.

However, even in this galaxy of stars, Phil Bennett stands out. He was to rugby what Botham was to cricket, Cruyff to football and Nastase to tennis. He had a certain magic, an indefinable quality. He had the audacity to attempt the unusual and to lift spectators out of their seats, as he did in Barbarians colours at Cardiff in 1973 when he instigated Gareth Edwards's famous try. Phil Bennett was simply phenomenal!

I hear those sceptics amongst you muttering, 'What does W.J. McBride know about outside halves? Wouldn't he be better off sticking to what he knows best!' And that, dear reader, is where you would be quite wrong. I don't profess to be an expert, no, but just because Max Boyce once waxed lyrical about that Welsh outside half factory, you think you have a monopoly on the position. Well, think again!

As a seven-year-old, growing up in Ulster, I was just old enough to remember Ireland winning the Grand Slam in 1948, and the excitement in Belfast when Jack Daly went over for the try that beat Wales 6–3 was something else. Those west Walians amongst you still romanticize the Llanelli triumph against the All Blacks in 1973, so you know how we feel when we relive that day at Ravenhill.

Ireland's Jack Kyle, one of the 'outstanding out halves', kicks for touch at Twickenham in 1957. (PA Images)

The star player in that 1948 Grand Slam team was Jackie Kyle who to this day is still held in the highest esteem by his peers (not least Phil Bennett himself).

And I've known other outstanding out halves: Micky English, Michael Gibson, Tony Ward, Ollie Campbell, Ronan O'Gara and Jonny Sexton for starters, all of whom have represented Ireland and the Lions with distinction over the last sixty years.

Whilst touring with the Lions in 1962 and 1966, I was lucky to play alongside Gordon Waddell, Richard Sharp and David Watkins. Talented as these guys were, for a variety of reasons the Lions never fulfilled their full potential. However, this state of affairs was overturned in 1971 when, with Doug Smith and Carwyn James in charge, we overcame the might of New Zealand to win the series. It did help our cause that we had 'The King' himself, Barry John, playing at fly half. We played some magnificent rugby on that tour with all fifteen players on the field contributing to never-to-be-forgotten performances.

In 1974, with Syd Millar now in charge, I was given the honour of captaining the Lions in South Africa. We had a strong squad, but among this talented group was one player who played as if he was from another planet: Phil Bennett. The sun-baked fields of South Africa provided the perfect platform for Phil to showcase his talents. Quick off the mark, he sidestepped and outstripped defences, but he could also kick the ball effortlessly all over the park. There was nothing this guy couldn't do! As a captain, you can only dream about having such a player in your team and what an inspiration he was to the other fourteen!

My entire playing career – Ballymena Academy, Ballymena R.F.C., Ulster, Ireland, the Barbarians and the Lions – has been spent in the pursuit of securing good ball so that the backs can do with it what they may. Strange as it may seem, when we get together today to enjoy a post-match Guinness, the talk is usually of the outside half!

To choose the 'Best Ever' in any sport is always a risky business. But when it comes to Llanelli and who should wear the number 10 shirt in the Greatest Scarlets XV Ever, there is no contest, no debate. There is only one name to be considered – Philip Bennett, and that is why I believe this excellent book has one glaring omission! But that omission is tribute to Phil's modesty. He should have let me pick the team!

According to Willie John, the sun-baked fields of South Africa in 1974 provided the perfect platform for yours truly, seen here giving Lions centre Dick Milliken something to chase at Ellis Park.

(Colorsport/Colin Elsey)

October 31, 1972, the day the pubs ran dry! All Blacks Lindsay Colling and Ian Kirkpatrick close down on me in the Stradey gloom.

(Colorsport)

Trying to dodge more Kiwis at Eden Park, Auckland, in 1977.

(Colorsport/Colin Elsey)

Introduction

> Bliss it was in that dawn to be alive
> But to be young was very heaven.

Even if the poet William Wordsworth probably had the Lake District in mind, these lines could also have been attributed to the industrial Felinfoel and Llanelli of the 1950s. Mine was a blissful and idyllic childhood, thanks to my warm and caring parents and a closely knit community where the round and oval balls reigned supreme – at least until summer came with its cricket contests and men in white V-necked sweaters plastered linseed oil on willow bats produced by Stuart Surridge and Gunn & Moore.

Thankfully there was no organised sport during my childhood. At Felinfoel Park it was a grab-a-ball-and-play philosophy; an hour of football followed by an hour of bruising rugby. The man who taught me to love sport as a boy was my father, Robert 'Bob' Bennett, and I admired him even more than my other sporting heroes – and they were all local, too! We were raised on legends and knew all about Jock Stein and Doug Wallace who had travelled all the way from Scotland to play for the Reds, namely Llanelli AFC. As a seven-year-old, I spent Saturday afternoons crossing Pen-y-gaer playing fields with my Dad to Stebonheath where the laughter and banter was truly infectious. Supporters congregated enthusiastically outside the Star Hotel where I, with a glass of lemonade in hand and match programme in the other, listened to tales of past encounters.

And when we played against Merthyr or Barry, the steep bank at Stebonheath would be jam packed and the roar of the home supporters enough to frighten the opposition into submission. Llanelli's fearless goalkeeper John Thomas was as mad as a hatter; he dived in front of opposing centre-forwards

This 1976 Llanelli pack of forwards don't seem particularly interested in my touchline conversion.

(PA Images)

with no concern for his own safety. He was also Dafen's wicket-keeper and I once saw him, fingers bent and twisted, stand up to Jeff Jones, one of the world's fastest bowlers, on the compact Welfare Ground.

When the Reds had an away match, Dad and I would go down to Stradey Park to watch the rugby. Although both of my parents were really hardworking (Dad at Llanelli Steel and Mam at Morris Motors) there wasn't much money left over for extras. This was true of most of the working classes of Llanelli at the time and it was why the matches at Stebonheath and Stradey were so well-supported. It was an escape from the rigours of everyday life.

Dad and I would make our way to Stradey along the railway track which ran through Felinfoel. This was an important line of communication between the anthracite coalfields of the Gwendraeth valley and Llanelli docks. It was not unusual to be joined *en route* by local workers who had just finished their Saturday shift at the town's steel and tinplate works.

As we walked in from Furnace Square, we were aware of a range of accents: the unmistakable Llanelli lilt, the beautiful sounds of the Welsh language spoken by fans from the Gwendraeth and Amman valleys, and the distinctive tones of Pembrokeshire were all squeezed into the ground, the classless community standing as one on the Tanner Bank, waiting patiently for kick-off.

The highlight of my afternoon was the blast of the referee's whistle at half time as I, along with hundreds of other enthusiastic youngsters, sprinted on to the playing surface in our quest for autographs. These giants of the oval ball, unlike the footballers at Stebonheath, also played for Wales and some for the British Lions! They included RH, Howard 'Ash', Ray Williams, Terry and Cyril Davies, Wynne Evans, Onllwyn and Carwyn. In those days there wasn't a hint of a technical talk at the interval; the players all grouped in a huddle, scoffed orange segments, took deep breaths, and signed a few autographs.

My first game of organised rugby was at Coleshill School when I represented 1A against 1B. It was all pretty chaotic but on the few occasions I got the ball I managed to evade the opposition with a few sidesteps to cross the try line. Our sports master, Mr Mervyn Bowen, must have been impressed because he told me at the final whistle, 'I'll have to keep an eye on you!' I ran home and with immense pride told my parents all about my first game. My mother's reaction was to go to wash my kit because she insisted I had to be dressed immaculately at all times.

When I look back at my career, there have been many wonderful moments for Llanelli, Wales, the Lions and the Barbarians. However, one of my top five rugby achievements involved Coleshill School Under 15's at the Llanelli School Sevens played at Stradey Park. Some of the schools represented were steeped in history: Cowley Grammar School, St Edward's Liverpool, Millfield, Halifax Grammar School, and Llanelli Grammar School. They were all masters of seven-a-side rugby. However, unfancied Coleshill got to the final in 1964 where we encountered the favourites, Bradford Grammar School. In shocking conditions we won 6–0 thanks to a 50-yard dash from our flyer, Chris Reed.

At that time Mr Bowen, our sports teacher, whom we all held in the highest regard, had been quite unwell and could not make it to the game so once the final whistle had been blown we all piled into teachers' cars and made the journey to his home to show off our trophy. We had won this huge cup for him – he had created an ethos in us boys which has remained with me throughout my career to this very day. I hope this comes across to listeners when I'm broadcasting. Yes, players have a duty to entertain and as Carwyn used to say, 'The most telling team-talk consists of just three words: Think! Think! Think!'

Phil Bennett
September 2014

Those posts at Old Deer Park looked a long way away when I was eighteen years old: London Welsh v Llanelli, 1967.

(Colorsport)

1976 at the National Stadium and I've managed to pick on someone my own size, France's Jacques Fouroux!

(PA Images)

Terry Davies, my Number One Llanelli full-back, kicks a conversion for Wales against Scotland in 1958.

(PA Images)

Chapter 1

15 FULL-BACK

For the best part of a century, the role of the full-back was crystal clear. The player who wore the No. 1 shirt (as it was until the 1960s) was the last line of defence. The early coaching manuals decreed that he should be the patient policeman at the back, taking responsibility for the high ball coming his way and accurately kicking his team out of trouble.

However, that manual had to be rewritten in the early 1950s when Lewis Jones, an eighteen year old from Gorseinon playing in his very first international and in front of an 80,000 crowd at Twickenham, decided to run from his own half and cause mayhem in a stretched English defence. With Malcolm Thomas and Bob Evans in support, Cliff Davies eventually plunged over for a magical try near the corner flag.

The subsequent match reports contained the usual analysis and jargon, but one term used was one for the future: counter-attack! Indeed all were agreed that in this instance attack had been the best form of defence.

Five months later Lewis Jones was the British Lions full-back playing against New Zealand at Eden Park, Auckland. The visitors were bravely defending their try line when Jones took a pass intended for his outside half, Jackie Kyle. With everyone at the famous venue waiting for the clearing kick, Lewis Jones decided to trust his instincts and following an outrageous dummy set off at blistering pace towards the halfway line. Bob Scott, the All Black full-back, was lining Jones up for the inevitable tackle, while Peter Henderson was cunningly shadowing Ken Jones on the wing. In an instant, having drawn the full-back, Lewis floated a pass over Henderson's head into the waiting arms of the Olympic sprinter, Ken Jones, to score unopposed.

The incomparable JPR Williams made the role of full-back one of the most influential in the team. Here he is about to put boot to ball watched by Peter Wheeler of England and another erstwhile Llanelli fly half, Gareth Davies. (Colorsport)

The exploits of the young Lewis Jones led to much head scratching from the coaches of the day. When New Zealand's Bob Scott and South Africa's Johnny Buchler also adopted a similar style of play, it heralded a complete rethink on the full-back's role. Indeed, by the time Monmouth School's Keith Jarrett calmly fielded a misdirected kick at the Arms Park in 1967 and sprinted half the length of the field to score a memorable try for Wales against England, the law book had long since been literally and metaphorically rewritten.

A new dimension was added in the 1970s by the incomparable JPR Williams, who could breach the opposing defence and create space for his fellow three-quarters with probing bursts. Ultimately, he made the role of full-back one of the most influential in the team.

Llanelli's Stradey Park was the stage for many world class full-backs. As a youngster, I never tired of hearing the old stagers singing the praises of the great All Black, George Nepia and maintaining that he was one of the best players ever in that position. 1998 saw another blistering performance from a full-back when Christian

'A masterclass in innovative rugby': New Zealand's Christian Cullen sees off Rupert Moon on his way to the third of his four tries at Stradey in 1997

(Colorsport/Peter Bush)

The resilient Roger Davies was a vital cog in the Scarlet machine.

(Colorsport)

Cullen scored four tries for New Zealand against the Scarlets – he gave a masterclass in innovative rugby which saw even the most partisan Stradey supporters on their feet in appreciation of such raw talent.

Gerwyn Williams from Glyncorrwg in the Afan valley represented Llanelli at full-back in the early 1950s. He was an extremely accomplished player who also played for London Welsh and became a PE master at Harrow School. He won his first international cap in the Triple Crown decider against Ireland at Ravenhill in 1950 and also played throughout the 1952 Grand Slam season. Williams also wore the No. 1 shirt in the last Welsh team to defeat New Zealand in 1953.

Another who beat the All Blacks was the resilient Roger Davies, Llanelli's full-back against New Zealand in 1972. Not a great kicker of a ball, he worked hard at his game and was a natural counter-attacker who suited the club's philosophy. In the 1970s, under Carwyn James's guidance, we wanted to become the Real Madrid of the rugby world and Roger was a vital cog in the Scarlet machine, and in our victory over the All Blacks the courageous full-back never flinched under the high ball. Llandeilo's Ian Jones, whose try in the 1990 Schweppes Cup Final against Pontypool was one of rare brilliance, was another full-back with flair. Pacy and unpredictable, he was Llanelli material through and through, but was one who left us wondering what might have been.

Circumstances and injuries also contributed to the early retirement of Adrian Lloyd who burst on the scene in the late 1960s. The Memorial Ground in Bristol was packed one Wednesday evening when Adrian and I played together for the first time. An outstanding talent, whose first instinct was to run with the ball, he broke through an organised defence that night and sprinted impressively for his try. At that time, however, rugby wasn't a career for someone so dedicated to his calling as a farmer and sadly he soon disappeared from the scene.

Others will remember Burry Port's Howard Davies, and of slightly more recent vintage, the Coslett brothers, Kel and Keri, the former signing for St Helens RLFC, where another Scarlets full-back would also later make his mark, namely Clive Griffiths, who gained his one cap for Wales as a replacement for J.P.R. Williams against England at Cardiff in 1979, before going north. And what of the versatile Kevin Thomas, whose development was ultimately hampered by a serious injury?

Who therefore tops the list as the best full-back to have represented Llanelli Rugby Football Club?

I first set eyes on Martin Gravelle at Aberavon on a blustery Wednesday evening in the late 1970s. The Talbot Athletic Ground is a tough place to visit, but it was so much worse on this occasion because several Llanelli players had dropped out prior to kick-off. Young Ashley Jones (Lyn Jones's brother) had been selected at open-side wing forward and I had memories of a sleepless night prior to playing against his father, Peter, a major tormentor of fly halves in the 1960s, whose tackles, even in charity matches, had 'cardiac arresting' written all over them!

'Who the hell is that bloke in the corner?' I asked as I made my way into the claustrophobic away dressing room. Martin Gravelle was a handsome young lad, but he looked as if he was still at primary school. That night, however, in only his second game, he was simply awesome. He had such soft hands and that innate ability to read a game and make the right decisions. Primarily a left-footed kicker, he also had the ability to stroke the ball stylishly and effortlessly for miles! He went on to play for Llanelli for the next eight seasons and I have no hesitation in saying that, had he possessed blistering pace, he would have gone on to represent Wales.

Bobby Moore at his peak was never the quickest but he had that presence. Martin Gravelle was of the same mould; he added finesse and flair to our attack. He didn't score many tries but he timed his entry into the three-quarter line with precision and with a perfectly executed pass created opportunities for others. He was also fearless in defence, dependable under the high ball and was always looking to counter attack. Everything about him was sheer class, and I consider him one of the finest full-backs to have worn the Scarlet jersey of Llanelli.

Incidenatlly, Martin was also a wonderful cricketer who played for the England Schools XI alongside future Test cricketers Paul Terry, Jack Richards and Dipak Patel. He went on to play for the Glamorgan Second XI and Llangennech as a free-scoring left-handed batsman and accomplished wicketkeeper.

I'm often asked, 'Who's the most gifted footballer you ever played with?' and I immediately answer, Ivor Allchurch. Whilst playing with him in many charity matches I just stared in disbelief at his ball skills and never stopped appreciating his ability to do the unusual and

Ivor Allchurch, the most gifted footballer I ever played with. (PA Images)

sometimes the utterly impossible with a football. Johnny Carey, the former captain of Manchester United and Ireland, once said : 'Playing against Stanley Matthews is like playing against a ghost.' Ivor was hewn from the same rock.

However, I'm absolutely convinced that Terry Price was one of the finest all-round footballers I was privileged to witness. Had Terry not suffered a series of crippling knee injuries and had he played for Llanelli or Leicester for his entire career, he would have been recognised the world over as a rugby sorcerer. Throughout his career he displayed an audacity on the field which made spectators leap out of their seats in wonder. His kicking skills were quite remarkable; his punts perfectly weighed and measured, his chips as precise as a top-class golfer's and his accurate goal kicking with the leather Gilbert ball enough to make opponents think twice before transgressing.

As a full-back coming into the line, Terry caused panic amongst opponents. The Scarlet Pimpernel of the back division, you never knew when or where he'd appear. We all recognised that the pulse of the game changed whenever or wherever Terry took possession; we were glad we played with him not against him! He was supremely confident in his own ability and had that arrogance (which all quality players seem to possess in abundance) to influence his teammates to deliver knockout blows to opponents. It's a team game, but individuals are often the ones who inspire others to expose the flaws. Throughout his career, even during his early days at Llanelli Grammar School, Terry Price had that capacity.

Don Clarke (left), another great All Black full-back, in the company of Wilson Whineray, whose 1963 touring team played a Llanelli team which included local grammar school boy Terry Price.
(PA Images)

Defensively he was the rock of Gibraltar, with the physique and mental strength to withstand challenges. Just imagine what it must have been like for him to step on to a packed Stradey Park to face Wilson Whineray's All Blacks in 1963 whilst still a pupil at Llanelli Grammar School. He must have had the nerves of a safe cracker because at half time he was asked to replace the injured Beverley Davies at outside half. But he adapted to the situation as if he were representing his beloved Hendy in a pre-season friendly. On one occasion towards the end of the match, acting almost by instinct, he crashed into the fiery Waka Nathan and accidentally broke the wing forward's cheekbone. The victory may have gone to New Zealand but the departing spectators sang the plaudits of the young schoolboy.

A few years later I remember an incident in a keenly contested match between the old enemies, Swansea and Llanelli, at St Helen's.

Following a slightly late tackle on Llanelli centre Mel Leach, I watched from a distance as both sets of forwards became involved in a kerfuffle in front of the main stand. It seemed as if things could well get out of hand but up stepped Terry to separate the warring factions. He just stood there in front of the Swansea players, his immense physical presence resulting in a peaceful conclusion.

In his younger days Terry was a superb seven-a-side player in the Llanelli Grammar School team which won the prestigious Rosslyn Park School Sevens on three consecutive occasions in the early 1960s. They beat all the top schools of the period and it was widely recognised that in a quite exceptional team Terry was simply immense. Following their hat-trick of wins, the powers that be withdrew their invitation in 1964 stating that the Welsh school smacked of professionalism with their individual track suits and meticulous attention to detail. I'll never forget his words of wisdom at the Llanelli School Sevens in 1963. He was standing at the touchline during one of Coleshill Secondary Modern's early round matches when we were a few points adrift. As I ran back to take the conversion following a try, Terry shouted, 'Phil *bach* – forget about the extra two points. You need time for another try!' He took an interest and understood the game inside out.

I remember travelling to Cardiff in 1965 as a sixteen-year-old to support Wales in their quest for their first Triple Crown since 1952. It was a filthy day with the Arms Park surface a sea of mud and after just five minutes Alun Pask, a truly great No 8 forward, was asked to play as an emergency full-back when John Dawes was injured. Terry Price spent the next twenty minutes in the centre but Wales, with their backs to the wall, performed splendidly and resisted all Irish attempts to crack them. Clive Rowlands's men thoroughly deserved their 14-8 victory with David Watkins and Dewi Bebb crossing for two vital tries. But it was Terry Price who was the Welsh hero. From the kick-off he called for the ball and with one torpedo kick sent the ball spiralling 65 yards downfield – he just oozed class. He went on to drop a magnificent goal from 45 yards and added a conversion and a penalty goal from the touchline.

In the late 1960s, my wife Pat and I were returning from Cardiff after a Llanelli fixture at the Arms Park. It was past closing time as we drove through Hendy (the M4 hadn't been opened) but I asked Pat to park the car outside the Hendy RFC clubhouse. I was dying for a pint

Hendy's Terry Price, 'the rock of Gibraltar', with the physique and mental strength to withstand all manner of challenges.

(Media Wales)

after a particularly hard encounter but was told in no uncertain terms that the bar was closed. And then Terry appeared – 'Open the bar, Phil wants a pint!' Only one man had the authority to take such action – not the Chairman, not the President, not the local J.P. but Terry!

I reiterate what I said earlier; the Hendy-born sports star was one of the finest rugby footballers I encountered first-hand. It's true that he never gave his body a break – he took part in so many different sports – and that this ultimately caught up with him. All in all, however, Terry John Price had it all.

One of the most respected rugby writers of the 1950s, 1960s and 1970s was former Welsh full-back Vivian Jenkins, whose distinguished sporting career included playing rugby for Wales, the Barbarians and the Lions, as well as first-class cricket for Glamorgan. Jenkins, who played in Wales's first ever victory at Twickenham in 1933, also had the distinction of being the first Welsh full-back to score a try in an international. In his excellent tome *Lions Down Under,* Jenkins chronicles the highs and lows of the British Lions's adventures in Australia and New Zealand. He pays tribute to the excellent performances of the two full-backs, Ken Scotland and Terry Davies, stating that both, of entirely different methods, were amongst the heroes of the four-month-long tour. According to Vivian Jenkins, the man from Bynea gave a superlative display, fielding everything impeccably, never faltering in the face of some fearsome head-on assaults and kicking a distance that put him in the Don Clarke class. He certainly was one of Llanelli's finest ever full-backs.

The 1960 Springboks proved to be an efficient outfit whose forwards were man mountains in ability and stature. They won 31 of the 34 games played, drawing with Midland Counties and France and losing only to the Barbarians at Cardiff. In the five international matches played they yielded just the one try, to Scotland's Arthur Smith.

Their 21-year-old centre three-quarter Francois Roux was their most potent attacker. However, his flying, late tackles caused innumerable injuries to opposing players, and such methods made him unpopular throughout his career. He smashed into Alun Priday, the Cardiff full-back in the first match of the tour and then launched himself into Malcolm Rogers as the Swansea player kicked clear. The tiny full-back was stretchered off to the nearby Swansea General Hospital.

One of the most talented and courageous of players, Terry Davies kicks ahead for Wales at St Helen's.

(Media Wales)

BURRDA SPORT
STEELS
DORE
DORE

The latest Scarlets full-back to make his mark at international level is the resourceful Liam Williams, but he is struggling here to get away from Harlequins' Nick Easter (left) and Luke Wallace. He has the ability to become one of the Scarlets' finest full-backs

(Andrew Matthews/PA Wire)

Morgan Stoddart, like Terry Price before him, had to give up the game before he had fulfilled his potential. A raw talent! So authoritative, so creative!

(© Huw Evans Picture Agency)

He continued to leave a trail of shattered individuals around Britain but came off a bad second at Stradey Park on December 13th. Terry fielded a high ball and instantly saw Roux closing in on him. Expecting a high challenge the Bynea man held his ground and swung into Roux ferociously knocking him to the ground. He was concussed as a result of the incident and missed the next game against Ireland in Dublin. It certainly taught him to be a little more selective with future tackles.

Leeds once offered Terry Davies a record £8,500 fee to turn professional but he remained loyal to his roots – one of the most talented and courageous of players.

But which of the two Terrys to choose? Unbelievably Terry Price only played 29 games for the Scarlets (and eight for Wales) before signing professional terms with Bradford Northern. Injury and rugby league robbed us of the best of the Hendy legend. Terry Davies, on the other hand, was captain of Wales and a lauded British Lion. What's more, he played around 140 times for Llanelli over six seasons, and he is my eventual choice to wear the No 15 shirt in my team of greats – but it was a close call!

Terry Davies dives emphatically over the line to score at the Gnoll.

'Dedicated professional in an amateur era',
Ieuan Evans takes the game to Leicester.
(© Huw Evans Picture Agency)

Chapter 2

14 & 11 WINGS

There are some sporting moments which are unique: the cover drive that wins a test match, the acrobatic volley that sends the ball flying past the goalkeeper into the corner of the net, or the sight of the wing three-quarter weaving his way to the try line. These are the moments that create the magic and draw the crowds.

I can still remember being taken to Stradey Park as a young lad to watch the stars of the 1950s and 1960s. A particular highlight was when the early season guest teams played the Scarlets in a midweek match: Gerwyn Williams's XV, Air Commodore Ranji Walker's XV and the Irish Wolfhounds were quality teams in their day and included many star players. Arthur Smith, who captained the Lions in South Africa in 1962 (and who also played for Ebbw Vale) and Peter Jackson from Coventry were two such players. And, as I watched from

Peter Jackson of Coventry, England and the Lions, whose sidestep and swerve of the hips created such magic in the 1950s and 1960s.
(PA Images)

the terraces, it was Jackson with that sidestep and swerve of the hips who created such magic!

The idol of the era, however, was Tony O'Reilly. I was fortunate enough to watch the Irishman play on more than one occasion, and the moment he ran onto the pitch the adrenalin began to flow through my veins. It was like watching Richards, Lara or Tendulkar stride out to bat. There was an aura about him: his self-confidence and good looks made him look like a superhero to a young boy. It is a wonder that MGM or Warner Bros did not sign him up for the latest Hollywood blockbuster!

O'Reilly, along with Cliff Morgan and Jeff Butterfield were the stars of the Lions tour of South Arica in 1955. The Irishman was also a superstar out in New Zealand in 1959. Even today, with all the big names that have subsequently worn the coveted red jersey, O'Reilly is spoken of as one of the greatest.

Stradey folklore also has its share of immortal wing three-quarters, like the remarkable Ernie Finch who joined the Scarlets in the early 1920s after impressing for Pembroke Dock Quins. He was soon winning international honours and faced Cliff Porter's undefeated All Blacks at St Helen's in November 1924 when Wales were outclassed by George Nepia et al. Ernie's big moment came four days later, however, when the All Blacks travelled west to Stradey Park. During this era, it was the wing three-quarter who threw the

'Idol of the era' Tony O'Reilly looked like a superhero to a young boy. Here he is seen returning from the Lions tour of New Zealand in 1959 with a Maori souvenir.
(PA Images)

ball into the lines-out and on one occasion that afternoon the ball was returned bullet-like into the waiting hands of Ernie Finch. He took off like a greyhound and sprinted towards the New Zealand try line. There was only one player standing between Ernie Finch and immortality. One of the greatest ever full-backs in world rugby, George Nepia, takes up the story.

> Rumours have been circling that when Ernie Finch scored he was so scared that he stopped dead in his tracks and when I went through with my tackle I missed him! The truth is different. At the critical moment Ernie swerved towards me, breaking my speed and my timing. He then swerved outwards again and by the time I regathered my composure, Ernie had scored a superb try.

This cameo ensured Ernie's place in the annals of the club's history.

I had also heard my father and his contemporaries talk about Elvet Jones and Bill Clement who both toured with B. C. Hartley's British Lions to South Africa in 1938. Indeed Elvet nabbed a try against the Springboks in the third and final test at Cape Town and finished as the tourists' top try scorer. He was considered one of Wales's real speed merchants, scoring 129 tries for Llanelli in a distinguished career.

Bill Clement from Felinfoel terrorised defences in the 1930s with his speed and sidestep. His vision as a rugby player was such that he could score and create tries: at Twickenham in 1937 Tanner and Davey combined to free Clement who, as he was being tackled, managed to slip a delicate scoring pass to Wooller. He would also create a try out of nothing against England the following year, chipping through for Idwal Rees to score. His career came to an abrupt end during that 1938 Lions tour when he suffered a serious knee injury. In due course both Bill Clement, a Second World War military hero, and Elvet Jones became powerful and influential administrators and I was privileged to have known both during my playing career.

Whenever Scarlets supporters discuss wing three-quarters, the name Les Williams inevitably crops up. Born in Mynydd-y-garreg, he created quite an impression at Stradey Park, winning national selection against England at the Arms Park in January 1947. The following season he joined Cardiff. During Les's first year, Bleddyn Williams scored 36 tries, but the great man was always quick to point out that Les Williams also crossed for 34 that year. He was the hero

Bill Clement, top try scorer and administrator.

(PA Images)

Les Williams kicks ahead on his international debut in 1947. Two years later he would score two tries in Wales's first victory over England after the Second World War.
(PA Images)

of Wales's first victory over England after the Second World War, scoring two tries at the Arms Park in January 1949. However, he created quite a stir a few days later when it was announced that he would join Hunslet Rugby League club for £1,450.

'Les was ideally suited to the 13-man game,' said his colleague Bleddyn Williams. 'He was fast, extremely skilful with ball in hand, a deadly tackler and a great finisher.' When he retired from rugby in 1956, Williams was appointed assistant director of physical education for the Cornish Education Board and spent 25 years in the county, eventually being awarded the freedom of Falmouth for the help he gave to sportsmen and women. It was there that I met him in the late 1980s. I had retired but whilst on holiday in Cornwall duly decided to join in his pre-season fitness routines and in due course Pat and I were invited for tea and scones at his home. I feel proud to have known him.

Two wing three-quarters dominated the Stradey scene in the 1950s – Ray Williams and Geoff Howells. 'Slippery', 'cunning' and 'swift' were some of the adjectives used to describe Ray's style of play and he proudly wore the scarlet jersey on 450 occasions, scoring 213 tries. There is an amusing story about Ray and the former Wales and British Lion centre D. Ken Jones and the time they were partnered together in midfield for Llanelli against Nuneaton on Easter Saturday 1960. At the time Ken was a sixth-form pupil at Gwendraeth Grammar School, where Ray was his sports master. During a typical Ray Williams break upfield, Ken was heard to shout politely:

> '*Syr, Syr… Pasiwch hi mas nawr!*' ('Sir, Sir… Pass it out now.')

Ray was a particular hero of mine and the local schoolboys always had the utmost respect for him. He was tall and distinguished and oozed class as a player and as a man. He lived in Felinfoel and even returned to play for his village club upon retirement from the first-class scene. I vividly remember one club match at Stradey when a long-distance Terry Davies kick at goal struck the upright. Ray Williams was the only player to give chase and duly scored an opportunist try. To borrow Grav's phrase, 'Top man!'

Elusive and fleet-footed, Geoff Howells of Loughor represented Wales throughout the 1957 season and featured with Ray Williams, for the first and last time, against France at Stade Colombes where Geoff claimed one of the four Welsh tries in a 19–13 victory. It was to be the last Welsh win in Paris for 14 years. I particularly remember one Saturday afternoon when I was amongst a throng of Llanelli supporters paraded in scarlet who had made the journey to St Helen's for a typical derby encounter. It certainly was a memorable match. Within minutes a clinical Carwyn James break supported by Cyril Davies, Dennis Evans and full-back Terry Davies released Geoff Howells who sprinted enthusiastically for the posts. Our never-to-be-recovered flat caps were thrown into the air as we returned victorious 5–3.

Deadly finisher Ieuan Evans is too quick for Nigel Walker as he squeezes in to score during a 1995 clash with Cardiff at Stradey.

(Colorsport/Cowie)

A few years later Robert Morgan from Pontyberem, another Gwendraeth Grammar School pupil, made his mark on the Welsh scene, and I still have great memories of sitting on that brick wall on the Tanner Bank at Stradey in the early 1960s watching this handsome, pacy, sinewy athlete beating opponents with a timely swerve and a change of pace, as he would later do for Cardiff also.

In the mid-1960s, eleven Felinfoel Youth players – Gerald Roberts, Gareth Thomas, Roger and Robert Fouracre, Stuart Gallacher, David Prendiville, Eric Watts, Brian Butler, Mike Francis, Roy Mathias and myself, represented the Welsh Youth team. At the time Roy Mathias was an outstanding wing forward, his resilience and stamina made him a formidable opponent. He was a nightmare to play against. He just lined them up and smashed them to the ground! He couldn't kick for love or money but when he joined Llanelli Carwyn James decided to convert him in to a wing three-quarter. He was an instant success. His powerful frame, coupled with speed off the mark, made him an awesome sight on the rampage. I well remember one try against Swansea at Stradey Park when he counter-attacked from his own 22. In front of a packed house the red-haired Mathias tore through the visitors' defence to be faced by the All Whites full-back, Dennis Lewis. Roy weaved inside and then veered outside, leaving the defender grasping thin air. The crowd were on their feet in

'One of the truly great Llanelli players', Andy Hill, a picture of tongue-tied concentration, gets his pass away against the Harlequins at Twickenham in 1976.

(PA Images)

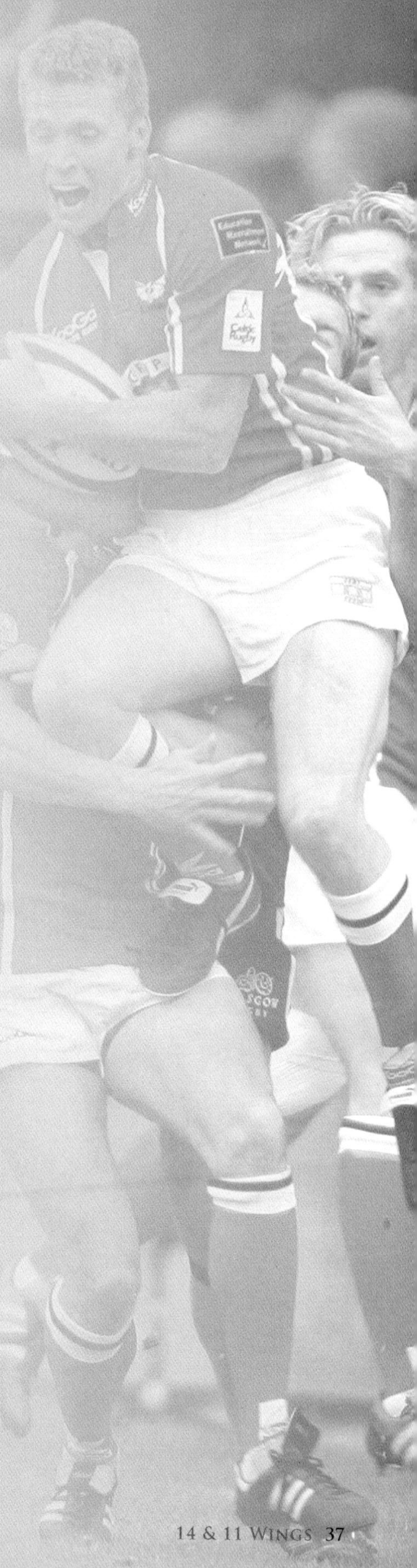

appreciation. He was capped against France in 1972 and then joined St Helens RLFC where he became a cult hero.

I've always been a great admirer of Andy Hill, one of the truly great Llanelli rugby players. During his time at Stradey Park he was a dedicated club man who always gave his all to the cause – he was never injured and wanted to play in every match. If anyone deserved to wear the red jersey of Wales, it was Andy but somehow in trial matches and during vital encounters when national selectors were present, the bounce of the ball never quite favoured him. In a final trial match at Maesteg, the man from Penlan, who was a prodigious kicker of a ball, missed his five kicks at goal! It was Norman Gale who brought him to Stradey and initially Andy found it very difficult to make his mark. He'd played soccer in the Swansea leagues and was a sprinter in the off season with the Swansea Harriers. However, he was determined to succeed, worked hard at his game, took on board the criticisms and soon became the idol of the Stradey faithful. Andy was one of the first round-the-corner goal kickers and became a points machine extraordinaire. In a total of 454 games for Llanelli he amassed 2577 points, which included 310 tries.

Hill's final game for Llanelli was in 1979, and as he walked off the pitch at Stradey for the last time he was asked whether he felt some disappointment at not having played for Wales despite such a successful career with the Scarlets. His reply speaks volumes for the man's character. 'Yes, I am a little sad, but playing here for twelve seasons in a team that produced such breathtaking rugby has been much more fulfilling than winning one cap whilst representing another team.'

At his peak in the mid-1970s, J.J. Williams was one of the top three wingers in world rugby and was recognised throughout the rugby-playing community as a lethal finisher. He took to the game like a duck to water; he played outside half for Wales at Under 18 level, had great hands and although he played most of his international rugby on the left wing he was equally at home on the right where his pace and cultured right foot caused problems for opposing defences. His chips and kicks were weighted to perfection and when Gareth Edwards or Selwyn Williams kicked long for position, JJ sprinted 50 yards to put pressure on the opposition. He played four test matches on the right wing; two for the British Lions against New Zealand in 1977, one for Wales against Australia in 1976 where he claimed a hat-trick

Never mind wizard's audacity, J.J. Williams finds himself in a tight spot at Cardiff in 1976 as France's Jean-Claude Skrela closes in. Meanwhile, his support players, Gareth Edwards (left) and Steve Fenwick seem a long way away.

(PA Images)

(it was only the second occasion in post-war rugby for a Welsh player to score three tries in a match) and the famous Grand Slam decider against France in Cardiff in 1978 where the Nantyffyllon flyer, hemmed in on the touchline, nonchalantly hurled the ball inside one-handed enabling me to dive over for a crucial try. And let's not forget that out in South Africa in 1974 he was simply sensational!

Though electrifying speed and a wizard's audacity were the trademarks of one of rugby's truly great wing three-quarters, he wasn't half a moaner on the field of play! What's more, he was always conscious of his facial appearance! He was once set upon in Newbridge when he received a bang on his nose. 'It's only a scratch, John,' said Bert Peel. But when he viewed the damage in the dressing room mirror he nearly strangled the Llanelli first aid man.

There is no question that Ieuan Evans is one of Llanelli's finest wing three-quarters. Although he was often starved of possession at national level, the Llanelli faithful witnessed some truly outstanding performances from Ieuan during the early 1990s, when the Scarlets proved time and again that they were one of the best club sides in Europe. I well remember the Salford University student making his debut for the club and making an incisive run which left the opposition in his wake. From the outset he proved that he was a deadly finisher and all-round footballer. Put simply: he had it all!

We all remember his solo try against England at Cardiff when he relentlessly chased Emyr Lewis's kick – other mortals would have given up the ghost, but not Ieuan. And in 1992, the world champions Australia were well and truly fooled when Colin Stephens and Simon Davies's scissors movement allowed Ieuan to steam through for a vital try. His horrific injury against Cardiff could have been career

George North, the giant with quick feet, creating Heineken Cup havoc for the team he would later join, Northampton Saints.

(PA Images)

ending, but Ieuan's resilience, courage and pride in performance came to the fore and he returned with a determination which was an example to sportsmen the world over. One still marvels at his magnificent individual try against Scotland in 1988 when he evaded five would-be tacklers in a remarkable sidestepping staccato run to the posts. Others regarded him as an opportunist *par excellence* best exhibited for the British Lions in Australia in 1989 when he pounced on a David Campese error to score a series-defining try in the third test at Sydney.

George North could turn out to be one of the sensational wing three-quarters in world rugby. The North Walian born in East Anglia plied his trade in west Wales for only a short period and the Scarlets, it has to be said, didn't see the best of him. However, for Wales, the British Lions and currently Northampton, the giant with quick feet often creates havoc.

Mark Jones, scorer of never-to-be-forgotten individual tries, leaves Munster's John Kelly in his wake during the 2007 Heineken Cup quarter-final at Stradey Park.

(David Davies/PA Wire)

There were others who caused breathless gasps at Stradey Park and beyond: Peter Rees, former chairman of the club, who played for Wales on two occasions in 1947; the other Terry Davies, whose performances were limited in number but who was one of the fastest rugby players I ever played with or against. Welsh international Carwyn Davies from Llangadog was a constant threat on Llanelli's left wing during the late 1980s and early 1990s. He crossed for 121 tries in 159 appearances including 45 tries in 44 appearances during season 1987-88. There was also Phil Lewis, a gliding runner with silky skills; Wayne Proctor who was the darling of the terraces for more than a decade – a balanced runner and modest young man whose impact on the team's attacking style cannot be overstated; Mark Jones whose exceptional pace resulted in some never-to-be-forgotten individual tries (if only the team had provided him with more ball during their Heineken Cup semi-final appearances); the underestimated Garan Evans, who could have walked from his home in Penmynydd to Stradey Park and whose try at St Helen's must rank in the top ten Scarlet tries of the century.

Wayne Proctor, 'darling of the terraces for over a decade'.

(PA Images)

The varied characteristics of wing three-quarters could form the basis of an interesting essay for PhD students – the breathtaking brilliance of Shane Williams and David Campese; the power and strength of John Kirwan and Jonah Lomu; the lightning pace of Bryan Habana; the sidestepping genius

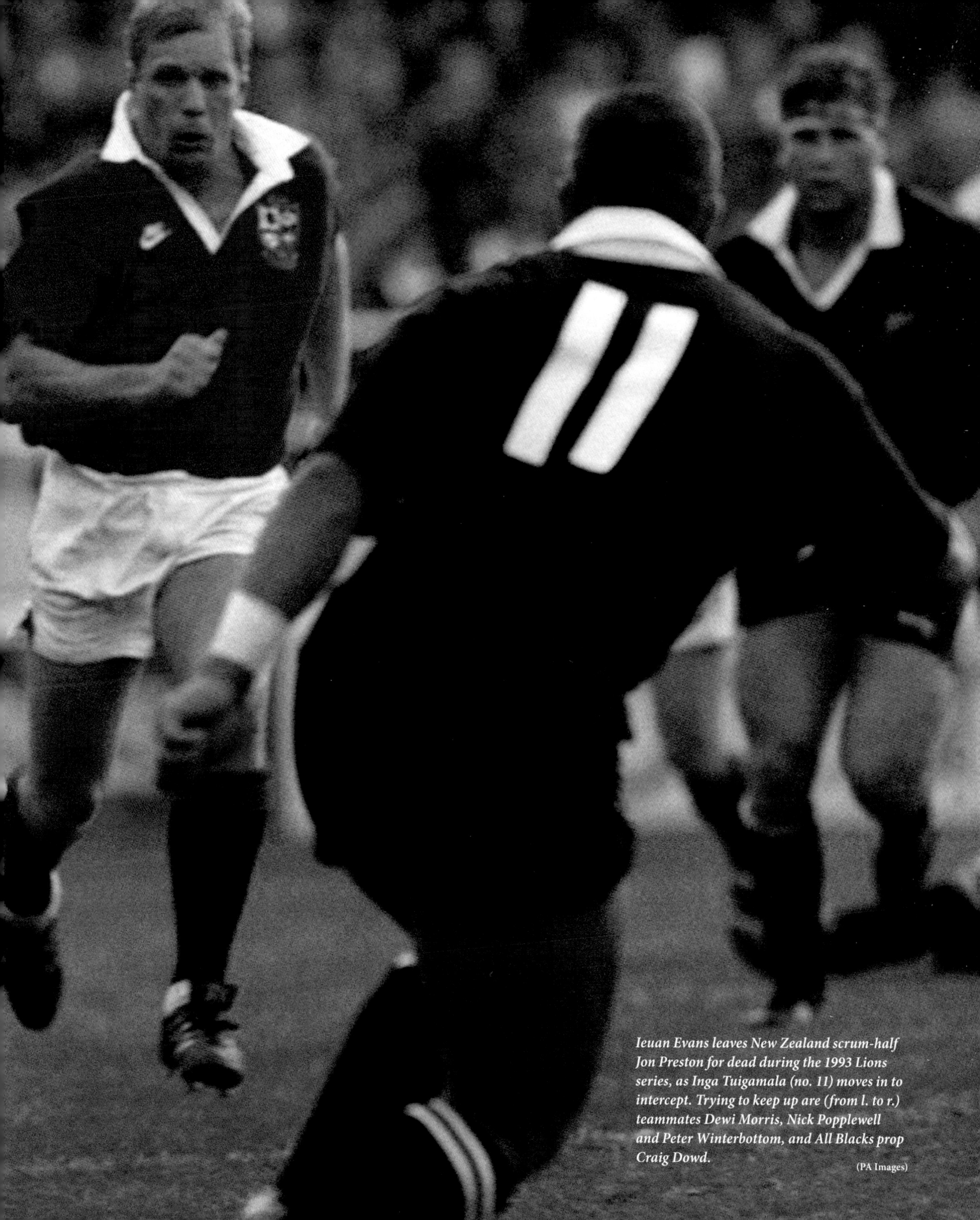

Ieuan Evans leaves New Zealand scrum-half Jon Preston for dead during the 1993 Lions series, as Inga Tuigamala (no. 11) moves in to intercept. Trying to keep up are (from l. to r.) teammates Dewi Morris, Nick Popplewell and Peter Winterbottom, and All Blacks prop Craig Dowd.

(PA Images)

exhibited by Israel Folau. I was privileged to play with and against truly great wingers, amongst them Brian Williams, Gerald Davies, David Duckham, Maurice Richards, John Bevan, Stuart Watkins and Keith Fielding. However, I have to say that the collection of Scarlets wing three-quarters in this chapter would more than satisfy me in a XV made in heaven. But I have to choose two!

Because of their sustained excellence with Wales and the British Lions, and because they both enjoyed success for the Scarlets against major touring teams, I have gone with J.J. Williams and Ieuan Evans. And who would argue with their Scarlets statistics: JJ scored 159 tries in 205 club appearances, whilst Ieuan scored 193 times in 231 games. I rest my case!

Who knows what the future holds? In a reprint of this book in twenty years time, Scarlet supporters might well be clamouring for the inclusion of Jordan Williams in a Greatest Scarlets XV Ever. The young wing three-quarter is a raw talent who constantly excites fans with a sleight of hand, a burst of speed, a magical sidestep and a touch of arrogance which we associate with true greats.

WINGS 11 & 14

JJ's hands are too quick for Springbok Klippies Kritzinger at Port Elizabeth during the third test of the 1974 series, as fellow Lions Roger Uttley (left) and Mervyn Davies continue in support.

(Colorsport/Colin Elsey)

Tinplater, centre, superstar: the one and only Albert Jenkins.

Chapter 3

13 & 12
Centres

Centre three-quarters have always been centre stage, often centres of attraction and in many cases centres of excellence, too. And whilst the position has always been open to all sorts, the job description continues to stipulate that the centre be both an accomplished tackler and a withstander of tackles, preferably nimble on his feet and prepared to put his body on the line.

A Samsonian physique seems always to have characterized one of the two centres in each team. Albert Jenkins, Claude Davey, and Wilfred Wooller, for instance, were all candidates for the pre-war Mr Universe title, and their robust style of play is still evident in today's game, having been passed down from the likes of Jack Matthews, Arthur Lewis, Ray Gravell, Scott Gibbs and John Devereux to Wales's current incumbent, Jamie Roberts.

Clermont-bound Fox and Hound: Jonathan Davies about to give international teammate Alex Cuthbert the slip at Parc y Scarlets.

(Huw Evans Picture Agency)

If these are the battering rams of the back division, then they are complemented by the flair of their partners, those who, with a sudden sidestep or swirl of the hips, can send the wing three-quarters away on a try-scoring run. These are the artists, the ones who tear up the script and create moments of magic in an instant. Think Bleddyn Williams, Gareth Griffiths, Lewis Jones, Cyril Davies, Malcolm Price, Mark Ring and Rhys Gabe. Born in Llangennech, Gabe was part of a famous quartet of three-quarters who distinguished themselves for Wales in the first decade of the twentieth century. Willie Llewellyn, Gwyn Nicholls, Rhys Gabe and Teddy Morgan will forever be remembered for the part they played in Wales's historic victory against the All Blacks in 1905 – it was Gabe who straightened the line and put Teddy Morgan in for the game's solitary score. He also made the crucial tackle on Deans in the never-to-be-forgotten disputed try. A fine defensive player, he was also one of the finest attacking players of his day featuring mainly for Cardiff although he was a Llanelli player when he was first capped against Ireland at St Helen's in 1901.

Four Welsh international Scarlets of the 1920s and 1930s:
Bryn Evans, Edgar Morgan, Albert Jenkins and Bryn Williams

(c. Ernie Griffiths)

The word 'superstar' is a recent addition to the Oxford English Dictionary. First credited to Frank Patrick in reference to the Vancouver Millionaires ice hockey teams of the 1910s–1920s, it became firmly established in the British vernacular after the musical *Jesus Christ Superstar* hit the West End stage. Soon it became an everyday term to describe the likes of George Best, Ian Botham, Gareth Edwards, Johan Cruyff, Vivian Richards and Bjorn Borg, or today Lionel Messi and our very own Gareth Bale and George North.

The word might not have been used at Stradey Park in the 1920s but Albert Jenkins was still a superstar! He was a heroic figure in the town and it wasn't unusual for a large body of fans to congregate hours before a match just to catch a glimpse of the great man as he arrived. Such were his superstar qualities that if, by some quirk of fate, Albert could not play because of injury or work commitments, the supporters would leave in droves and spend the afternoon in local hostelries.

'I'm playing with Albert!' was the cry when Rees Thomas read in *The Llanelli Mercury* that he had been selected to represent the Scarlets on their Easter tour to Cornwall. It certainly was a dream come true for the young wing forward because, whilst everyone in the area wanted to play for Llanelli RFC, running out onto the field of play alongside Albert was the ultimate accolade. Albert was as glossy and well-built as a racehorse and amongst his many qualities was the ability to change the course of a match. The first occasion Albert appeared in the scarlet jersey was against Neath at the Gnoll where spectators were given a foretaste of what was to come when Jenkins produced one electrifying run of some fifty yards. Encouraged by what they had seen, they would subsequently turn up in their thousands to witness Albert produce one superb performance after another. At the end of the 1919–20 this is what *The Evening Post* had to say:

> There is a rugby footballer at Llanelly called Albert Jenkins. He is a tinplater by trade, and in his spare time, since he returned from France a few weeks ago, after long service, he wins matches for Llanelly by kicking goals and scoring no end of tries. The bigger the match, the better he performs. He is worshipped by the Llanelly crowd, half of whom are attracted week by week simply to see Jenkins display his skill. He is as good as Rhys Gabe at his very best, and everybody who has seen him play knows this, except the Welsh Football Union. But news travels fast, and there is a

> more active body in control of the Northern Union. They have heard of Jenkins's ability and attempted to get his signature long ago without success. They are determined to get Jenkins. One Northern Union player said they were going to get him whatever the price. The news of the offer soon got about Llanelly and a warm reception was threatened for any Northern Union men who prepared to offer Jenkins further inducements to go North and a local boxer (Billy Roberts) is said to be keeping a watchful eye for any strangers in the camp.

Lewis Jones: 'he did things that no one else could'.

(PA Images)

Professors Dai Smith and Gareth Williams in their excellent *Fields of Praise* (University of Wales Press, 1980) take up the story :

> He [Albert] had certain specialities for which he was unrivalled. He could punt or drop-kick half the length of the field with either foot; he was adept at taking the ball one-handed at speed; he evoked admiring shouts as with miraculous agility he rolled over and bounded up when knocked down… At 5 foot 8 inches and 12 ½ stone, his barrel chest and squat, stocky frame made him look shorter than he was, but those muscle-packed proportions tapered down to sprinter's calves, narrow ankles and small, balletic feet. No ballet dancer, though, could have tackled like Albert…

Listening to the older generation back in the 1960s in Felinfoel was an education for us youngsters. They all agreed that Albert carried Llanelli single-handedly and as a result the whole team rallied round him. There was an aura about him which remains to this very day. I would have loved to have seen him play.

A few years ago, at a Wooden Spoon Society function in Belfast, I was privileged to meet Jack Kyle. He achieved fame as one of Ireland's Grand Slam heroes of 1948, a fly half who later became recognised the world over as a result of his exploits on the Lions tour to New Zealand in 1950. As one journalist wrote,

> They seek him here, they seek him there
> Those Frenchies seek him everywhere;
> That paragon of pace and guile,
> That damned elusive Jackie Kyle!

He was such a humble human being. He insisted the lunch be called 'The No 10 Lunch' rather than 'The Jackie Kyle Lunch'.

He later became a doctor in some of the world's poorer countries and spent three decades in Zambia where he is still held in high esteem by the population, especially in the impoverished townships.

I spent some twenty minutes in Dr Kyle's company at that lunch organised by Willie John McBride to honour one of Ireland's finest. There were several outstanding outside halves present, including Michael Gibson, Ollie Campbell, Tony Ward, Micky Quinn, Alan Old and the great Cliff Morgan who spoke with passion about one of life's gentlemen via a video link from the Isle of Wight.

I was in awe of the man. When we started talking about Llanelli he recalled that Lewis Jones had played for the club and immediately

Wales's Roy Bergiers in complete control of the situation, as ever, against Ireland in 1975. (Colorsport)

started eulogising. 'What a player!' he said. 'I never knew a man like Lewis Jones; he did things that no one else could. Such flair; such genius. The opposition were scared of him; they just couldn't cope with his unpredictability. If he had stayed in rugby union he would have challenged the greats. Phil, that man Lewis Jones – he was years ahead of his time. Outrageous! How dare he! Unbelieveable!'

Within a few months of that 1950 Lions tour, Wales lost him to the professional code as Leeds Rugby League Football Club finally got their man. Within months he was the golden boy of the thirteen-a-side game. At a prestigious dinner in Leeds a few years ago I was honoured to meet some of Yorkshire's sporting icons, amongst them England cricketers, Olympic medallists, international footballers and rugby league stars. As each of these was introduced to the 500 guests, thunderous applause ensued, but when the names John Charles and Lewis Jones were read out, the audience rose as one, as if to royalty, in recognition of their very special talents. I was so proud, so close to tears.

When I was a primary school supporter of the Scarlets, one of my favourite players was the well-built Cyril Davies (he of the white bandage around his forehead), and in the playing fields around our home I used to copy his style of play, always carrying the ball in two hands. It was a joy to witness him timing his pass to perfection and, if coaching DVDs had been produced in the 1950s, then it was Cyril who would have conducted the masterclass. I would say he was in the same league as John Dawes, Phillipe Sella and Regan King. He played his final game for Wales against England at the Arms Park in January 1961 when he created two glorious tries for Dewi Bebb (Wales won 6-3) before leaving the field early in the second half with a burst blood vessel.

In the early 1960s Llanelli fielded several centres who all wanted to wear the No. 10 jersey, of those none stood out like D. Ken Jones. I remember one occasion when he received the ball near his own goal line, nonchalantly sidestepped his opponent and found himself in acres of space. With a smile on his face he changed gear and sprinted the remaining 75 yards to the try line with others in hot pursuit, an act he was to repeat in a never-to-be-forgotten try for the British Lions against the Springboks at Ellis Park in 1962. Another of that era who combined speed and sidestep was Brian Davies: in today's game he would have been a lethal finisher on the wing.

Roy Bergiers was a wonderfully talented player whose physique was ideally suited to the demands of centre three-quarter play. A top class athlete, Roy excelled defensively, could pass the ball beautifully and always seemed to be in complete control of the situation. When we left for South Africa with the British Lions in 1974 I thought he would have been the number one centre but a knee injury cost him dearly, allowing Ian McGeechan and Bob (Dick) Milliken to make the most of their opportunities. Roy seemed to epitomise the amateur ethos of the past; he was a true gentleman and one of the nicest blokes I ever played with. However, in the heat of the battle he was a hard uncompromising individual, ever reliable, exhibiting great skills when others around him often faultered. The centre partnership he forged with Ray Gravell has become part of Stradey Park legend. Theirs was an almost telepathic understanding, each complementing the other in their styles of play. He was also the man-of-the-moment in our historic victory against New Zealand in 1972 – his pace, determination and bravery resulting in a vital try on that unforgettable afternoon.

Unique! One off! Man in a million! The late Ray Gravell, the man mountain from Mynydd-y-garreg, remains a cult hero here in Wales. The Irish just loved him, but he was also highly regarded throughout the rugby-playing community from Dumfries to Durban and from Dunedin to the banks of the Dordogne. Rugby has always been a contact sport; today it can be described as a collision sport, and Grav would have revelled in such an environment. It was my privilege to have played with him at club and international level and therefore be in a position to assess his many talents. With ball in hand he could be a bone crusher as he bulldozed his way through opponents. However, he could quite easily play the role of the midfield playmaker, speeding past would-be tacklers before handing the ball gift wrapped to supporting players.

We first met at Stradey Park in an early season training camp when Carwyn decided to stage a full-on contact session. I took possession, made a run, and felt confident until Ray appeared from nowhere and dumped me on the ground. I was flabbergasted. Then he had the audacity to pick me up, and smiling like a Cheshire cat, apologised for the inconvenience! That was my introduction to Raymond Gravell!

Man in a million, the late Ray Gravell, is oblivious to my plight as he sweeps the ball on during the Welsh Cup quarter-final against Pontypool in 1975. Right behind him is his midfield partner-in-crime, Roy Bergiers.

(Colorsport/Colin Elsey)

Ray Gravell demonstrates his footballing skills, kicking ahead for Gerald Davies (no. 14) to chase at Twickenham, 1976. The Englishmen in pursuit are (from l. to r.) Peter Squires, Martin Cooper and David Duckham. (PA Images)

Yes, there was only one Grav, but that individual contained several Gravs. Grav the rugby player, Grav the broadcaster, Grav the sword bearer in the National Eisteddfod, Grav the family man, Grav the film star, Grav the Welshman who loved his country with an undying passion.

The Scarlets of the 1970s knew, however, that Ray lacked confidence. His pre-match preparations were part of a ritual that the great man had to perform to prepare himself psychologically for the encounter. Players, even referees, were grabbed by the throat and interrogated: 'Who is the best centre in Wales?', 'Who is the strongest centre in Wales?'. 'Who is the most creative centre in Wales?' And the answer we invariably gave him was 'You Ray!'

I can remember him pacing around the visitors' dressing room at Stradey Park one afternoon like a caged lion, asking those same old questions of his teammates. Later, some ten minutes into the game, a scrum formed on the halfway line, and the ball shot out into Grav's hands. Eyeing the tiniest of openings, the bearded wonder weaved his way past the two Bridgend centres, raced downfield, drew his opponent and passed the ball to the supporting J.J. Williams. A score was inevitable! However, the Scarlets had not reckoned on the speedy response of Bridgend's J.P.R. Williams who launched himself

Allan Lewis, a top coach, but who knows how good a player he would have been had injury not ended his career so cruelly and prematurely? (Huw Evans Picture Agency)

A British Lion by the age of twenty-one,
Peter Morgan seemed destined for great things.

(Colorsport/Colin Elsey)

Nigel Davies, so typical of the gifted footballers produced by the Scarlets over the years.
(PA Images)

at JJ as the wing three-quarter plunged over for the score. In some discomfort, JJ limped back. He was in obvious pain. The first to arrive was Ray. 'Quick, get Bert Peel [the trainer]. I've hurt my knee. The reply was pure Grav. 'Yes, yes, yes, JJ. All in good time. But who's the best centre in Wales?'

Today, the buzz word in the rugby world seems to be *analysis* and even the youngsters who play for WRU academies are provided with DVDs and asked to pay particular attention to their opponents' strengths and weaknesses. It was so different in my day when we were told to concentrate on our own game. But I distinctly remember the one occasion, whilst representing Llanelli Schoolboys against Amman Valley Schoolboys, our coach drilling us in the dressing room: 'Watch out for their inside centre, Allan Lewis, who could be a threat.' And he was! A beautifully balanced runner and a magnificent passer of the ball, he went on to represent Loughborough Colleges and whenever available, Llanelli, where I played with him on several occasions. I was in close proximity when Allan, at the age of 21, broke his leg against Swansea at Stradey Park in 1970, an injury which ultimately ended the career of a guy who would have gone on to play for Wales. Such is life.

On Fridays in the 1970s, sales of *The Guardian* newspaper quadrupled in Llanelli and west Wales. Even diehard red-top readers, which included most of us players, would go up-market to see what the maestro Carwyn James had written in his weekly column. It was always a gem of in-depth analysis and I remember one occasion the paper's sports editor had asked six leading journalists to pen articles about their players of the future. Carwyn decided to write about Peter Morgan, a shy, gutsy young man who had just joined the Scarlets after impressing for the Welsh Youth XV and in early season trials with his accurate kicking out of hand, fine distribution skills and ability to cut defences to shreds. When he first arrived at Stradey Park (and I played with him for two or three seasons) we were somewhat taken aback by his Mediterranean tan and good looks. His brightly coloured car with a surf board planted on top confirmed his status as a man of the ocean and he often exhibited surfing techniques on the rugby field, riding the opposition waves effortlessly!

The underrated Dafydd James, a test-match try scorer for the Lions in Australia in 2001, shows the Wallabies a clean pair of heels.
(PA Images)

By the age of 21 Peter had played for Wales, the Barbarians and toured with the British Lions to South Africa in 1980. However, he suffered setbacks at vital stages in his career: an indifferent

Stradey royalty: Regan King untroubled by Wasps Danny Cipriani and Mark Van Gisbergen during his first spell with the Scarlets (David Jones/PA Wire)

performance at outside half against Ireland at Lansdowne Road along with a severe leg injury severely dented his confidence.

Other centres who captivated audiences at Stradey Park over the years were David Nicholas, Peter Hopkins, Neil Boobyer, John Thomas, Cyril Evans, Dennis Evans and Billy Upton. And what of the underrated Dafydd James whose achievements as an international winger (for Wales and the British Lions) are a testament to his dependability and unfailing judgement?

An indispensable member of the great Scarlets XV of the early 1990s was Nigel Davies whose intuitive timing of the pass led to tries galore for Messrs Proctor and Evans. Next to him stood Simon Davies, strong, hard and deceptively quick over the first ten metres. Likewise Leigh Davies, who arrived at Stradey Park with 21 caps via Neath, Cardiff and Bristol, and became the region's first captain in 2003, often partnered by a real jack-in-the-box in the form of Matthew J. Watkins.

Regan King only represented New Zealand on one occasion, but he is blessed with the kind of subtle wizardry which brings the

Easy Pisi! Scott Williams evades Northampton's George Pisi at Parc y Scarlets. (David Jones/PA Wire)

A high, high jump for huge joy! Former Scarlets centre partnership Jonathan Davies and Scott Williams celebrate Jonathan's try against the team he would later join, Clermont.

(Huw Evans Picture Agency)

grandstand to its feet. Not the quickest centre maybe, he still manages to squeeze between opponents before flicking the ball into the waiting hands of a teammate. He has returned for a second spell with the Scarlets, and who knows he may again be the catalyst for a brand of rugby manufactured in heaven.

The new millennium has also seen the Scarlets continue to produce outstanding homegrown centre three-quarters. Jonathan Davies and Scott Williams have been ripping defences apart with a blend of midfield play reminiscent of the true greats of the past. Jonathan at a tender age is being hailed as one of the finest centres in world rugby and his presence in the Clermont midfield alongside Wesley Fofana will undoubtedly make him one of the hottest properties in the oval game. He was one of the stars of the successful Lions team which toured Australia in 2013 and whilst the exclusion of the great Brian O'Driscoll from the final Test caused astonishment in some quarters, the young man from Bancyfelin handled it all with dignity and ended up receiving all the plaudits at the end of the match. He has certainly blossomed from a novice into an outstanding talent.

Young Scott Williams's explosive style reminds me of Jonathan, and he too seems to be progressing magnificently at regional and international level. With the bulk and pace to succeed, Scott is a skilful and silky centre who varies his angles of running intelligently and is certain to scale the loftiest heights of the game.

But who will represent Phil Bennett's Greatest Scarlets XV Ever? I am impressed with the latest generation of centres, but I am conscious of the word 'Ever' in the title of this book. Whilst I never saw him play, I cannot resist the testimony of my father and his friends, and a legion of Scarlets supporters down the years who were brought up on the legend of Albert Jenkins. And to partner him? It is impossible to stand in the way of the irresistible force that was Ray Gravell. w

13&12 CENTRES

The irresistible Ray Gravell, in Lions colours.
(Colorsport)

Stephen Jones: an all-round outside half of immense talent.

(Huw Evans Picture Agency)

Chapter 4

10

Outside half

No team in the history of European rugby has produced as many gifted outside halves as Llanelli Rugby Football Club. Though the advent of the professional game has ushered in major changes, the role of the fly half remains crucial. The number ten is still the man who controls play and has a decisive say in the running of the game. Of late, the man who's made the job look easy is the All Black maestro, Daniel Carter. He doesn't run, he glides. He doesn't kick the ball, he strokes it effortlessly into space. When Carter takes possession, not only does the pulse rate of the game change but also that of the spectators.

Llanelli's first capped outside half was John G. Lewis who played his one and only international against Ireland at Birkenhead Park in 1887. Dai Morgan and Ben Davies were regarded as pioneers of the scrum and fly half system of half-back play and according to the

The ultimate in modern fly halves, New Zealand's Daniel Carter, weaves his way past Wales's Adam Jones (left) and Lee Byrne at Dunedin in 2010. (PA Images)

Llanelli Mercury, 'They have been the smartest pair of halves in South Wales,' and Morgan represented Wales on two occasions in the late 1880s.

Dai John was an inspiration to the Scarlets in the 1920s. He received lavish praise on a regular basis in the back pages of the *Mercury* : 'a real marvel at stand-off', 'no other player can extricate himself from difficult positions with such dexterity', 'his screw kicks to touch are the admiration of all'. Dai played five matches for Wales during the 1923 and 1928 seasons and the press throughout Wales were adamant that he should have played more games for his country. In fact Dai Smith and Gareth Williams's *Fields of Praise* stress the fact that Dai John and Albert Jenkins were consistently overlooked by the selectors. Indeed when Dai John was not picked for the 1926 game against Ireland, the WRU received 200 angry and abusive letters with 199 bearing the Llanelli postmark.

Three fly halves deserve special mention for inspiring performances against Southern Hemisphere touring teams. A dropped goal by Ron Lewis enabled Llanelli to lead until the last minute of play in a heroic struggle against the touring Wallabies in 1947, during which Australian forward Colin Windon was dismissed by referee Ivor David of Neath. Les Phillips also succeeded with a dropped goal against the 1951 Springboks in an uncompromising encounter won by the visitors 20–11. Les was a real gentleman and in conversation never mentioned the fact that he had played against visiting tourists. Jeff Tucker featured at fly half against the All Blacks in 1953, crossing for the home's side solitary try. Apparently he was a fine reader of the game with good hands and a decent turn of pace.

One of my boyhood heroes, however, was the Llanelli and Wales fly half Carwyn James and little did I know at the time that the great man

Many forget that Carwyn James was a fine player before he was a fantastic coach. Here he receives the Russell-Cargill Memorial Cup as London Welsh's captain at the Middlesex Sevens in 1956. (PA Images)

Still King of New Zealand, Barry John made his name at Llanelli before moving to Cardiff.

(Colorsport/Colin Elsey)

would have such a bearing on my rugby life. He formed breathtaking partnerships with Wynne Evans and Onllwyn Brace, and the crowd loved his sleight of hand, jinking runs and calculated decision making. He was born in the mining village of Cefneithin where the whole community was obsessed with rugby. It was unfortunate for Carwyn that Cliff Morgan dominated the Welsh rugby scene in the 1950s, especially after his unforgettable performances for the Lions in South Africa in 1955.

As a coach, Carwyn James was ahead of his time and when he returned triumphantly from the 1971 Lions tour of New Zealand he could well have been canonized. He could have coached great club and national teams the world over but he decided to remain faithful to Llanelli Rugby Football Club. An exceptional coach, he was also a prolific writer and an eloquent broadcaster with a razor-sharp intellect. As his friend and fellow journalist Frank Keating says in his book *Up and Under*, 'Carwyn, with his blend of romance and pragmatism, remains a prophet round the world.' Carwyn's philosophy is as pertinent in the modern game as it was back in the seventies. It still prevails at Parc y Scarlets and it's a legacy which would have made him a proud man.

As a Glamorgan cricket supporter, I have to include the multi-talented Alan Rees. He was not only a fine middle-order batsman and brilliant cover point, but also an outside half whose distribution skills and balanced running brought him three international caps in 1962 before he departed for Leeds RLFC.

'Genius' and 'legend' are accolades which should be used sparingly in any field. However, Barry John was both these things. One of the finest fly halves in the history of the game, Barry reminds me of Daniel Carter at his very best, which is praise indeed. During the 1971 tour of New Zealand he tore the All Blacks to shreds when his play caused as much astonishment as admiration. The Lions backline with John Dawes and the mercurial Mike Gibson in midfield simply destroyed the opposition. V.H. Cavanagh, who, in his time, was one of the greatest coaches in the world, stated after his first sight of John, 'Barry John is the only rugby player I have ever seen who can beat a man without moving his feet.'

I was a contemporary of Barry, of course – a few years younger but nevertheless well qualified to make an assessment of his qualities. I was playing youth grade rugby at Llanelli when Barry arrived at Stradey Park and I was in awe of him. He had an aura, an air of indifference and languid charm which endeared him to teammates and opponents alike. He respected his fellow players and, even when we faced each other in fierce derby matches after he had left for Cardiff, we always had a high regard for each other.

I still remember my first Llanelli-Cardiff encounter. Captain Norman Gale had worked us up to fever pitch: back-rowers Alan and Clive John were all set to mark and nullify their brother Barry, and it promised to be a real humdinger. Cardiff were a great side and when they duly arrived with Gareth, Barry and Gerald wearing their lavish suits and Baa Baas ties, it seemed as if their confidence was flowing. It proved a torrid affair which we managed to win 9–0. I was constantly hounded and threatened by the marauding John Hickey, whilst the John brothers somehow managed to keep Barry on a tight leash.

Gwyn Ashby from Tycroes was an extremely gifted fly half who played most of his rugby for the Scarlets in the centre alongside the pocket dymamo and outstanding sevens player from Glanaman, John Thomas. Gwyn was one of the nicest men I ever played with and without doubt the finest exponent of the dummy I encountered. In training we all knew it was coming, but he seemed to fool us time and time again. When the Scarlets came within a hair's breadth of defeating the mighty Springboks at Stradey in 1969, several of us were prevented from playing by our international commitments. Step forward, Gwyn Ashby, however. And though Alan Richards and Brian Butler scored the tries, it was Gwyn at outside half who controlled the game majestically, and in today's man of the match culture would have walked away with the champagne!

Llanelli born and bred Bernard Thomas was an immense talent. (Colorsport)

Llanelli born and bred Bernard Thomas was an immense talent – an all-round footballer with a siege-gun kick out of hand. At fly half, his opportunities at Stradey Park were limited, but when he moved across to play centre, he displayed deft touches and was a constant threat. His time at Aberavon proved beneficial and even today the Talbot Athletic Ground faithful readily recall his adventurous running and vision. Bernard represented Wales 'B' during the 1973–74 season and proved himself a key tactician when the Scarlets narrowly defeated the visiting Maoris in November 1982, enabling them to emulate the success of the Llanelli teams of 1888 and 1926. I was privileged to watch Bernard in action on many occasions when I reverted to full-back to allow him to play in his natural position at outside half.

When Geraint John of Haverfordwest first appeared for Llanelli in the early 1980s, I honestly thought he was a future international in the making. He was an elegant runner and superb kicker, however he never quite fulfilled his potential when there was an opportunity to make a name for himself. Llanelli's performance against Swansea just a few days after Carwyn died was truly inspirational with Geraint displaying the flair and panache that the master coach had come to expect from his team.

Gareth Davies was another outside half from the Gwendraeth Grammar School conveyor belt. He had an ability to lean back and make the ball talk and I have to say that he was one of the finest kickers of a rugby ball I've ever seen. Some might say that he lacked pace but he made up for it in so many other areas. His control at number ten was quite masterly and had he stayed in west Wales throughout his career, I have no hesitation in saying that he would have been a Stradey great! His departure for Cardiff was inevitable as a result of university commitments. He formed with Terry Holmes one of the finest club half-back partnerships in European rugby at the time.

If ever a player had faith in his own ability, it was Laugharne's Gary Pearce. He might have played his best rugby for Bridgend but he soon became a favourite at Stradey Park with his infectious smile and outrageous dummies. Hard, determined and a superb controller, he had the knack of leading back-row forwards up blind alleys, making teasing half breaks before releasing supporting players into space. Gary's contribution to Llanelli's magnificent 19–16 win over the touring Australians in 1984 was a telling one; his try, three penalty goals and a conversion proved decisive in a remarkable victory. He will forever remain in Stradey folklore, however, as a result of his magnificent injury-time winning dropped goal against Cardiff in the 1985 Schweppes Cup final. When he took possession he was some ten metres in from the near touchline and some 30 metres from the posts but somehow managed to propel the Gilbert oval high into the air and between the uprights.

It was Meirion Davies who told me all about Jonathan Davies. 'Come and see this pupil,' said the Llanelli hooker and Trimsaran Primary School teacher after one training session at Stradey. I went along and marvelled at the eleven-year-old's magical skills. He had everything – determination, aggression, a sidestep which bamboozled the opposition, electrifying pace and a love for the game. He was undoubtedly destined for greatness. Years later he somehow slipped

'Come and see this guy!' Trimsaran's finest and Great Britain full-back, Jonathan Davies, accelerates past the Kangaroos defence at Wembley en route to one of the greatest tries scored in either code of the game. (Colorsport)

through the net at Stradey Park but the canny Brian Thomas spotted his talent and drafted him into the Neath squad. The Welsh All Blacks became a force to be reckoned with and with Jonathan at the helm the team won plaudits for their style of football.

The call came on a Sunday morning from the Neath supremo: 'Phil, your favourite outside half has injured his knee and as you know I've got a memory like an elephant. I remember you telling me that your back problem was sorted out by a top orthopaedic surgeon from west Wales. Have you got his telephone number?' Within days Jonathan was examined and treated by Maldwyn Griffith and was back playing in record time. He played brilliantly for Neath and the diehard supporters still reminisce about his superlative solo tries against Bath and Bridgend. However, storm clouds hovered overhead. He received a stream of virulent letters when he transferred to Llanelli; his time at number ten for Wales was clouded in controversy after some heavy defeats to New Zealand and an embarrassing reversal against Romania. Jonathan desperately wanted to address members of the Welsh Rugby Union about the lack of professionalism in the game but his pleas went unanswered. It came as no surprise when it was announced in 1989 that he had joined Widnes Rugby League Club for a fee of £230,000. It was a massive blow for Welsh rugby as he had so much to offer.

He enjoyed a glittering career in the professional code, although initially targeted by opposition – 'We'll murder him!' remarked Andy Gregory – but unfortunately they couldn't catch him! He became a hard man who totally destroyed his opponents and it was no surprise when he was voted Rugby League's Man of Steel after some match-winning performances for Warrington, Wales and Great Britain in 1994. The pinnacle of his career was the try he scored for Great Britain against Australia at Wembley. With the game building towards a dramatic climax Jonathan received the ball near the halfway line running past one defender before swerving on the

No. 10 Colin Stephens leaps highest as Ieuan Evans scores against the world champions Australia at Stradey in 1992. Ieuan is kneeling in prayer, whilst Lyn Jones (no. 7) and Rupert Moon join the chorus of adoration. (Colorsport)

The most professional player I have ever come across: Stephen Jones, typically combative as Osprey Justin Tipuric tries to bring him to ground.

(Huw Evans Picture Agency)

outside to avoid two or three more. In front of him was Brett Mullins, acknowledged as one of the fastest men in world rugby. He slowed down for an instant and then accelerated outside Mullins for the try line. It was one of the greatest sporting moments Wembley has ever witnessed. To this very day I'm so proud that a boy from the mining village of Trimsaran had succeded in such a cut-throat sport. His community and his family meant everything to him and I have no hesitation in saying that Jonathan Davies was a true rugby great.

Colin Stephens will forever be associated with one of greatest victories ever achieved in the club's history. The visitors in late 1992 were the World Cup holders, Australia. Even the most optimistic supporters recognised that the task ahead was a daunting one. The Wallaby side selected was a strong one but the Scarlets, under the shrewd coaching partnership of Gareth Jenkins and Allan Lewis, were no respecters of reputations. The catalyst for Llanelli's only try was Colin Stephens. It was a move perfected on the training field – the fly half with ball in hand feigned on two occasions to release teammates and in the process created a huge void for Ieuan Evans who received the ball at pace and darted over near the posts. With a minute left the scoreboard read : 'LLANELLI 9 AWSTRALIA 10'. And then the coup de grâce – Colin deaf to the desperate calls of his centres attempted a drop goal. It was poorly struck but the ball somehow, for all its questionable trajectory, scraped over the bar. The outside half added another drop goal for good measure.

The classy Frano Botica was instrumental in Stephen Jones's development.
(Colorsport)

Colin Stephens was the typical Welsh outside half – dimunitive, cheeky and arrogant. I've always had a huge rapport with the family – as a young lad his father Brinley was a Felinfoel hero who had given devoted service to the club. Whilst still a youth player I was selected to play in the centre for the first team in an end-of-season friendly against Aberavon Green Stars where I was asked to mark former Swansea star John Simonsen. Brinley quickly dispelled any pre-match butterflies by saying, 'You leave him to me, Phil!'

I trained with Colin in the early 1990s and although I had been banned from the premises for writing a book, I changed in my car and accompanied conditioning coach Peter Herbert and the team for pre-season training. I was impressed with Colin's pace off the mark. He was lightning quick over short distances but his legs seemed to turn to jelly once we'd run a hundred yards. Colin was a precocious talent but seemed to lack confidence in his own ability.

Frano Botica oozed class. I'd appreciated his talents during his time at Wigan RLFC who at that time were one of the finest teams I'd witnessed in any sport. His contract nearly bankrupted the Scarlets but his professional attitude and 'winning is everything' mentality rubbed off on players and coaches alike. He was so instrumental in the development of young Stephen Jones, passing on useful tips to the young apprentice at every opportunity. I well remember the players exiting for a shower after training sessions, leaving Botica and Jones out on the playing arena. His vast experience was a real bonus to the club; he'd possibly lost a yard of pace but was still a superb controller at number ten. He represented the All Blacks on 27 occasions and would have won many more caps had it not been for the goal-kicking excellence of Grant Fox.

Stephen Jones (right) and Jonny Wilkinson contest the ball during the 2003 Rugby World Cup quarter-final.

(PA Images)

I have to say that Stephen Jones is probably the most professional rugby player I have ever come across. Somehow he always had to prove himself; the so-called experts on national television often criticised him describing him as manufactured and mechanical but those who doubted him had to rethink. When Wales enjoyed their renaissance in the 2003 Rugby World Cup against New Zealand and England, it was Stephen Jones who led the attack. Again it was his counter-attack from deep which proved the defining moment in a great comeback victory against France at the Stade de France in 2005. In my estimation he was an all-round outside half of immense talent, a magnificent team player who managed to make himself a hot property in the modern game. Undoubtedly Stephen was one of the bravest fly halves I came across, often playing behind beaten packs but more than prepared to do the donkey work associated with back-row forwards. His time at Clermont allowed him to develop and mature not only as a rugby player but also as a man, and it was in the hot beds of Toulouse, Perpignan and Castres that he learnt to deal with hostile atmospheres and crowds baying for blood.

Llanelli's Stephen Jones tackles his fellow scoring machine, Neil Jenkins of Cardiff, during the 2000 European Cup quarter-final.

(PA Images)

His partnership with Dwayne Peel for Llanelli, Wales and the British and Irish Lions was an instinctive one; Peel's rocket-like service allowing Stephen time and space to dictate play. They'd known each other over a long period of time, practised together constantly and talked endlessly in Welsh which must have flummoxed the opposition. Possibly the main weapon in his arsenal was his kicking ability, but unlike many of his peers he seemed comfortable on either foot. He was, along with Jonny Wilkinson and Neil Jenkins,

Rhys Priestland kicks for goal.
(Andrew Matthews/PA Wire)

the premier scoring machine of his day, notching 970 international points along with 2850 points in the Llanelli jersey. The final word goes to Neil McIlroy, Clermont's analyst for the past twelve years: 'Not only is he a truly great player but a magnificent ambassador for Wales.' Personally, I have no hesitation in saying that Stephen Jones was an absolutely outstanding player for the Scarlets who is up there with the greats of the club.

Is it Biggar or is it Priestland? It's the debate which has caught the attention of the rugby public in Wales in recent times. Rhys Priestland is a delightful man, polite and unassuming who could possibly do with more faith in his own ability. Certainly his decision to remain with the Scarlets is a boost in trying times and I have no hesitation in saying that he will be a positive influence during the next few seasons. He's got it all in his locker as he proved during the 2011 Rugby World Cup. On his day he can be outstanding, whether sticking meticulously to a pre-arranged game plan for his country, or controlling instinctively for his region.

Another fly half who slipped through the net is Leicester's Owen Williams, who hails from Ystradgynlais. His stay at Parc y Scarlets was a short one but is most certainly destined for a successful career. A fine distributor, he also rifles the ball accurately with both feet and what particularly impresses me is his attitude – if he misses a kick at goal it doesn't bother him in the least.

Of the above I have to say that three stand out – Barry John, Jonathan Davies and Stephen Jones. Barry will forever be mainly associated with Cardiff, Wales and the Lions, whilst Jonathan proved himsef a rugby league phenomenon. However my vote for the outside half position in the Greatest Scarlets XV Ever goes to Stephen Jones whose total commitment to the club and region will endear him to all supporters.

10 OUTSIDE-HALF

'A magnificent ambassador for Wales'. Stephen Jones is determined to break Wynard Olivier's tackle during the final test of the 2009 Lions series in South Africa.

(PA Images)

Dwayne Peel, whose genius brought colour to dismal Saturday afternoons.

(Huw Evans Picture Agency)

Chapter 5

9

Scrum half

Wales has always produced world-class scrum halves. As far back as 1905, Dickie Owen, a boilermaker by trade, from the Hafod in Swansea, put his engineering skills to good use to create Teddy Morgan and Wales's match-winning try against the All Blacks. Back in the early decades of the 20th century, Owen was a great thinker on rugby football and especially scrum half play:

> My idea is that the scrum worker, directly the ball is heeled, should pass direct and as swiftly as possible to the stand off man... To do this... a swift and accurate pass should be given from a stooping position... If you're going to pass, do so at once, and from the very spot where you get the ball.

The 1920s saw Wick Powell from London Welsh lauded for his performances whilst 1935 was a vintage year for Haydn Tanner.

Whilst still a sixth-form schoolboy, he was drafted into the national side following a five-star performance for Swansea against Jack Manchester's All Blacks and played an important part in Wales's defeat of the touring side. The line of notable scrum halves is a long one and includes such well known names as Rex Willis, the immortal Gareth Edwards, Terry Holmes, Robert Jones, Robert Howley, Dwayne Peel and Mike Phillips.

Interestingly though, in the period between 1881 and 1993, not one Llanelli scrum half managed to establish himself in our national team. Rupert Moon was the first Scarlet scrum half to gain more than ten caps for his country. Thankfully, over the last few years, there has been an upturn in fortune in this department. Dwayne Peel led the way with his 76 caps for Wales and three for the British and Irish Lions, whilst it must be remebered that Mike Phillips started his distinguished career at Stradey Park.

The warrior scrum half, Mike Phillips, charges at Wasps halfbacks James Brooks (no. 10) and the gloved Matt Dawson.
(PA Images)

As an outside half, I realise the importance of a swift and workmanlike scrum half. There are times when his role is a link between forwards and backs. This is when a swift, accurate pass from one half back to the other is the order of the day. Another situation demands a show of strength – this is when the poor fellow has to stand his ground and compete with a pack of marauding giants. Occasionally there will be a need to produce a well-executed box kick to relieve pressure or to test the defensive qualities of the opposition.

When Haydn Tanner withdrew from the Welsh side to face Australia in 1947 Handel Greville stepped into the breach and in tandem with fly half Glyn Davies orchestrated a 6–0 victory against the tourists. The fluent and combative scrum half from the Gwendraeth valley also played for the All Whites against South Africa in 1951.

Wynne Evans was born and bred in the close-knit mining village of Llandybie. He was closely involved in the coal industry, was a powerful and strong 'scrum worker' whose game typified his upbringing. A ninth forward who never gave a bad pass and would volunteer to take a hiding when things took a turn for the worst, he typified the west Walian scrum halves of his era and represented the Scarlets for nine seasons in the 1950s, captaining them during the 1956–57 season. He won his only international cap when he, along with five other Scarlets, including Carwyn James at outside half, were chosen to wear the red jersey against Australia at the Arms Park in January 1958. Wynne was the perfect foil for Carwyn, ensuring that the fly half had time and space to dictate proceedings. Wales won the match 9–3 but the half backs, who had performed admirably, had to make way for Cliff Morgan and Lloyd Williams for the England match a fortnight later.

I fondly remember spending a few hours in Wynne's company one Wednesday evening (or was it a Thursday morning?) in the 1970s. We were returning, in WRU President Handel Rogers's car, from a charity match at Lampeter. Several of us were desperate for a toilet stop and Handel suggested the conveniences at the Golden Lion in Llandybie, a public house owned by none other than Wynne Evans. It was way past stop-tap but we were welcomed with open arms by mine host and several of his regulars. We eventually emerged three hours later! The welcome was sincere and it was such a pleasure to be in the company of working-class people who knew and appreciated their rugby.

I have thrilling memories of seeing Onllwyn Brace playing for the Scarlets. In the mid-1950s, Onllwyn along with former England

To watch the enterprising Onllwyn Brace play was to be thrilled.

(PA Images)

cricket captain M.J.K. Smith, revolutionized Varsity rugby with their open, attractive style of play. The annual match between Oxford and Cambridge, played in front of a packed house at Twickenham, was usually a dog-fight with both teams trading penalty goals in attempting to achieve bragging rights for the next twelve months, but Onllwyn's philosophy was to avoid contact and employ skill to find space and score tries. He was way ahead of his time and according to the leading rugby writers of the day was the true embodiment of Welsh rugby – talented, innovative and enterprising. Though he was not the kind of scrum half who relished a wet and windy Gnoll on a Tuesday night, the images of Onllwyn masterminding victories are still with me: the bullet-like pass to Carwyn, who in turn would flick the ball over his shoulder to the supporting Onllwyn on a looping run. Genius, pure genius!

Dennis Thomas was the complete package: a combination of Wynne Evans and Onllwyn Brace. He was a boyhood hero of mine, a Roy of the Rovers idol to Felinfoel youngsters who simply adored the Scarlets. Dennis never flinched even when mighty All Black forwards (whether from New Zealand or Neath) bulldozed their way towards him. I came into the Llanelli side in 1966 partnering Dennis at half back and I still remember his comforting words prior to kick-off. With one arm around me he said, 'Phil *bach*, I'll look after you.' And he did! Clive Rowlands, one of Wales's great servants and who also started his career at Stradey Park, reminds one and all that Dennis was one of the best scrum halves he ever played against and that he should have represented Wales. He was a real handful and, to a young outside half hoping to make his mark in the game, it was comforting to know that I would always be more than an arm's length away from the scavengers of the day, like Alan Dix, Omri Jones or Morrie Evans.

Dennis Thomas was also one of the nicest gentlemen I ever came across and I hated letting him down. I well remember walking towards Eynon's team bus one Sunday morning outside the Petersham Hotel in Richmond. I was obviously worse for wear after sampling the local brew and felt guilty as Dennis uttered the never-to-be-forgotten words, 'You'll never learn!' He was from farming stock and lived on a farm near the Farriers Arms on the road from Furnace to Trimsaran, just a Terry Davies kick from Stradey Park. I was so proud to have played with him and both my sons were honoured to have been taught by him at Bryngwyn School in Llanelli.

Scrum halves from other countries weren't fit to lace Selwyn Williams's boots.

(Colorsport/Colin Elsey)

Australia's scrum half John Hipwell whips the ball away at Stradey during the 28–28 draw with Llanelli in 1976. The Scarlets looking on are (from the left) Hefin Jenkins, Selwyn Williams, Gareth Jenkins and Alan James.

(Colorsport)

Selwyn Williams was unquestionably the fittest individual I ever played with. The man from Clunderwen in Pembrokeshire also possessed a firecely competitive edge and, thank goodness, I never had to face him on the squash court where apparently he was a formidable opponent. His remarkable mobility was always in evidence, as he had that priceless ability to get the bad ball away from nigh-on-impossible situations, even at times chipping the ball into my waiting hands. Another time in another age and Selwyn would have represented Wales on thirty-odd occasions; he was never injured and to put it bluntly, scrum halves from other countries weren't fit to lace his boots. His omission from the Llanelli v New Zealand match in 1972 still hurts. It could have been the greatest moment of his life but he remained glued to the bench for the whole match. I wasn't involved in the selection process but it must have been a close call to include Ray 'Chico' Hopkins at No 9 – a decision which I suppose was vindicated because Llanelli won the match. However, Selwyn's presence at every reunion since 1972 underlines his value as a team member and says a great deal about his attitude and character.

I have fond memories of several other scrum halves who graced Stradey Park during my playing career and in the decade or so

'Seconds out.' Chico Hopkins (extreme right) decides to leave his Llanelli pack to it as tempers fray at Stradey on the day that New Zealand are defeated. Scarlets (left to right) are Derek Quinnell (clutching head), Tony Crocker, Hefin Jenkins (obscured), Gareth Jenkins (no. 7), Tom David, Roy Thomas (no. 2 on the floor) and Barry Llewellyn. Looking on is referee Mike Titcomb. (Colorsport)

following my retirement. Gareth Thomas was a schoolboy star who represented his country at Under 15 level and went on to play for the Welsh Youth. His opportunities for Llanelli were limited as a result of Dennis Thomas's presence but not to be deterred he joined the Wizards at Aberavon and earned his spurs with his accurate distribution skills and control. Chico Hopkins made only nine appearances for the club before departing for richer pastures in the North of England but his name will forever be etched in Welsh rugby history. He inspired Wales to a remarkable comeback victory against England in 1970; within minutes of replacing Gareth Edwards the Maesteg man had plunged over for a debut try which motivated the men in red to emerge victorious, 17–13. It was his only appearance for Wales but sixteen months later he again replaced Edwards, this time after seven minutes, for the British Lions in the first Test against the All Blacks at Dunedin in 1971. He again performed admirably linking effectively with Barry John in a 9–3 win. Again, it was his only Test appearance for the Lions. Chico had proved himself to be a big match player in difficult circumstances and it was this which endeared him to coach Carwyn James. Very few players are able to boast a 100% record in more than one encounter against New Zealand – Ray Hopkins was one of them.

Vernon Richards from Morriston was a versatile and wily scrum half who always seemed to have a smile on his face. A lovely man, as mad as a hatter, he was entirely at home on a rugby field. Although a Swansea Jack, he soon won plaudits from the Stradey crowd and I well remember the odd comment in the heat of battle as he made his way to a set piece, 'Pass all right, Phil?'

Mark Douglas was built like an ox, which was understandable as his father owned a slaughter house near Lampeter. He was from the same mould as Terry Holmes and David Bishop and often managed to keep the Scarlets in games even when our forwards were hopelessly ineffective. Mark had that presence on the field which resulted in opposing back row forwards showing maximum respect for him. Today's analysts with their costly laptops would have to devise intricate schemes to keep Mark Douglas in check!

Jonathan Griffiths was a brilliant sportsman with a great attitude towards the game. He could have played county cricket and in the

A scrum half to keep defences honest, Mark Douglas is about to hand off Scotland's Roger Baird at Cardiff in 1984.
(Colorsport)

Firefighter and livewire Jonathan Griffiths gets the ball away against Scotland at Murrayfield in 1989. (Colorsport)

current 20/20 format I daresay he would have attracted attention from the IPL in India. He was a prolific destroyer of opening attacks and loved to hit the ball well beyond the boundary rope. I well remember partnering Jonathan for Ronnie King's Fire Brigade XV against Llanelli in the late 1980s. I'd long since retired but kept myself in good shape and jumped at the chance of reliving the past. The match attracted a decent size crowd and with us firefighters fielding the likes of David Fox, Mark Perego, Anthony Griffiths and Jonathan Griffiths, it seemed the Scarlets would be in for a tricky contest.

It was meant to be a friendly, a fixture to raise funds for the local fire brigade, but throughout the match no quarter was asked and no quarter given. Playing outside Jonathan that evening was a real privilege; his service rapid and accurate, his work rate infectious, his commitment an example to his fellow players whilst his dynamic running caused mayhem in the home team's defence. I remember telling Ronnie aferwards that if Jonny Griff had been cast in *The Towering Inferno*, Steve McQueen could have taken a back seat! Oh, by the way, the Scarlets supporters left in disbelief as the firemen emerged victorious.

From the hundreds of players who have represented Llanelli over the years, there are a select few whose blood has deepened from red to scarlet, such has been their devotion to the club. One of these is undoubtedly Rupert Moon. Born and bred the other side of Offa's

Dyke in Walsall, Rupert's commitment to the cause was evident to all who watched him play and made him a much loved and much respected figure at Stradey. How, said the fans, could Neath have released a player of this calibre?

Gareth Jenkins, who was in charge at the time, rated him highly because in Rupert he had not only a ninth forward but also someone who could sweep the ball out to the backs quickly and efficiently. Another plus factor for Gareth was that Rupert did as he was told i.e. he followed the game plan and was no prima donna.

When Rupert was at his peak, I was in my fortieth year but still comparatively fit so when the invitation came to oversee or join in a coaching session, I was only too happy to accept. What stood out for me was how the partnership between Rupert and open-side wing forward Lyn Jones had developed into a telepathic one. During the previous match Rupert injured his shoulder after a particularly robust tackle and left the field in a great deal of pain. Bad news for him, but worse news for us because our next game was against the old enemy, Swansea and we wanted our best players available.

Come Saturday, who should lead out the team at St Helen's but Rupert Henry St. John Barker Moon! He put in a man-of-the-match

Handing off Matt Dawson, the only crumb of comfort for Rupert Moon on a heartbreaking afternoon at Reading as the Scarlets lose a European Cup semi-final to Northampton in 2000.

(PA Images)

Dwayne Peel, the real deal, takes on Daniel Carter during the first test of the 2005 Lions series in New Zealand.

(Colorsport/Kieran Galvin)

Combative and newly capped, Gareth Davies.
(Huw Evans Picture Agency)

performance which saw the Scarlets sneak an unexpected victory. If I had thought highly of him as a player before this encounter, then my admiration soared after what must have been a particularly gruelling afternoon for him. One other game which stands out for me is the victory against Australia in 1992. Health and safety standards today would have demanded that he leave the field halfway through the second half: he was apparently concussed following a blow to the head, but in true style he played on and helped secure the victory. He may not have been born to the west of Loughor Bridge but Rupert Moon will forever be recognised as a true Scarlet.

Mike Phillips's performances during Wales's 2008 and 2012 Grand Slam successes were quite inspirational, as was the pivotal role he played for the Lions in South Africa in 2009 and Australia in 2013. The warrior scrum half from Bancyfelin in Carmarthenshire started his first-class career at Stradey Park before becoming a rugby nomad, advancing his rugby development (and bank balance) by changing clubs at regular intervals, though he now seems settled in Paris with Racing Metro. Mike is a big man, physically robust, able to withstand fierce onslaughts but always able to read situations quickly and open up options for his team. His time with the Scarlets was relatively brief but he will always be remembered with great fondness.

Another of the Scarlets' international scrum halves, Rhodri Williams, scoring against Clermont.
(Huw Evans Picture Agency)

Playing outside Dwayne Peel would have been a personal dream ticket! His trademarks were his courage, his pass and a running game which caused panic in opposing defences. The number nine from Tumble in the Gwendraeth valley rose to prominence at Stradey Park in the early years of the current millennium, one whose genius brought colour to dismal Saturday afternoons. Within a season or two Dwayne had convinced the pundits that he was ready to scale the loftiest heights of the game. By heeding advice and practising tirelessly, he attracted the attention of the national selectors, winning his first cap for Wales in the bustling city of Osaka in Japan in 2001. He soon became a role model for scrum halves; he wasn't as muscular and powerful as Terry Holmes, didn't have Gareth Edwards's explosiveness, but his passing was of the highest standard. On a rugby field a second is an age and it is the scrum half's distribution which allows the outside backs that crucial second.

Dwayne was as two-footed a kicker as he was two-handed a passer, allowing him to dictate play subtly in defence and attack. He was quite superb on the back foot. Having played a leading role in Wales's

Grand Slam success in 2005, he was one of very few British and Irish Lions who returned from New Zealand with his reputation enhanced. Everything seemed to be falling into place for Dwayne but somehow his rugby career turned sour when he departed for the Sale Sharks. An individual who would surely have won more than a hundred caps for his country became the forgotten man. My great friends Fran Cotton and Steve Smith are mystified: 'He's the best scrum half we've ever had at Sale' and as far as I'm concerned he's the best scrum half we've ever had at Llanelli.

Which brings us to the Scarlets's current incumbents: the combative and newly capped Gareth Davies, the fleet-of-foot Rhodri Williams and the polished Aled Davies. Their future is a rosy one, I'm sure, but as far as the Greatest Scarlets XV Ever is concerned, no one is going to oust Dwayne Peel any time soon!

9 SCRUM-HALF

Dwayne Peel causing panic in the Glasgow ranks with his trademark tap-and-go. In support is Mark Jones, whilst a kneeling Scott Quinnell and Chris Wyatt are happy to lend moral support from a distance.
(PA Images)

Worth his weight in gold: Laurance Delaney.

Chapter 6

1 & 3
PROPS

Old school prop forwards saw themselves as the colliers of their day, and a shift in the front row could be as hard as anything endured by the miners in their cramped conditions underground. Modern exponents of the ancient art, however, need to be athletic: they spend hours in the gym, they run around the field like quarter milers, tackling anything that moves and are often seen taking the ball at pace in midfield! They continue to be the men-mountains they have always been, and continue to leave us wondering whether William Webb Ellis had scrummaging in mind when he started running with the ball at Rugby School in 1823!

Who am I, a mere outside half, to try to analyse the workings of the front row? There are generations of players who, even though they played in these positions, still cannot give a clear insight into who does what and to whom when it comes to scrummaging. It never ceases to amaze me how, when a scrum collaspes and the whistle is shrilled, the referee can speak with such authority on the subject as he lectures the perceived offender. I'm not going to pretend to be an expert on the scrummage but after listening to those who are (or who say/think they are!) and after reading up on the subject, I have my own list of great forwards who played there for the Scarlets.

Over the years, Llanelli has produced fine prop forwards, many of whom went on to win international honours, like Tom Evans from Ammanford, often described by sports journalists of the early twentieth century as being 'the finest forward Llanelli had ever turned out'. In an era when so many Llanelli players were ignored by the national selectors, it is worth noting that Tom won 18 caps for Wales, and became an automatic selection for his country for five seasons, playing in three Grand Slam XVs in 1908, 1909 and 1911. I wonder if there's a Tom Evans Road in Ammanford?

Archie Skym, born in Drefach in the Gwendraeth valley in 1906, first played rugby as an 18-year-old 'for something to do' during the coal strike. He was first capped against England in 1928 and went on to win 20 caps for his country. A policeman, he eventually moved to Cardiff after joining the Glamorgan Constabulary and along with Tom Arthur and Ned Jenkins became the bedrock of a Welsh pack that began to dominate in the early 1930s. Although acclaimed as a prop forward, he appeared in other positions in the pack as a result of his versatility and mobility.

John Warlow from Dafen initially played for Felinfoel before joining Llanelli during the 1957–58 season. He played against the 1960 Springboks in a one-sided affair dominated by the South African forwards. However, John continued to impress and won his only cap for Wales in the hangover match against Ireland at Lansdowne Road in November 1962 – a game postponed from the previous season because of a smallpox outbreak in the Rhondda. Within a matter of months, he decided to join St Helens Rugby League club, distinguishing himself for the Saints and later Widnes and

A rare honour for Prime Minister Harold Wilson at the 1966 Rugby League Challenge Cup Final: meeting John Warlow, ex-Llanelli prop forward. On his right are St Helens teammates Ray French and Alex Murphy.
(PA Images)

Rochdale. He also toured Australia and New Zealand with the Great Britain team and played in a Welsh team which defeated England at Salford in 1968, 24–17 – it was Wales's first league international since 1953 with former Scarlet Terry Price kicking six goals. A career highlight was undoubtedly the 1966 Challenge Cup Final at Wembley which pitted St Helens against their close rivals Wigan, a match which drew a capacity crowd of 98,536. The Saints won 21–2 and included two Welshmen in their line-up, loose forward John Mantle and Warlow. A week after defeating Wigan, St Helens completed the double by lifting the Championship after demolishing Halifax 35–12.

To this very day Howard 'Ash' Davies remains a Llanelli legend. Born in the Seaside area of the town and the son of a butcher, he was instantly recognisable as the thickset figure whose bandaged forehead was always covered in blood! He had some almighty battles with Gwyn Lewis from Swansea, and I remember one particular incident when both these fierce front-row forwards left the field at the same time to be stitched up. Yes, Howard Ash was a fiery individual but even today at Parc y Scarlets the supporters still remember him with fondness. He was a hard man who gave his all and will always be remembered as a great clubman.

On one occasion after a Saturday afternoon fixture at Bath, the Eynon's coach dropped the players outside the Town Hall Square near the Glen Ballroom late at night. Apparently one of the bouncers saw that Howard Ash was amongst the group and immediately ran around the building in a state of panic shouting 'He's on the bus!' I had the honour of delivering the eulogy at his funeral and just before I got to my feet his wife Betty said, 'You will say something nice about him, won't you?'

Stanley Matthews and Denis Compton were the sporting celebrities of the 1940s and 1950s, but my father hero worshipped the Llanelli and Wales prop forward from Burry Port, Griff Bevan. He was a big man but all through his life was known as a gentle giant. Along with twelve others, he won his only cap on the losing side to England in the first official international match after the Second World War. The great Bleddyn Williams also made his debut, not at centre but at outside half, where he looked out of place and where he would never play for Wales again! It was Griff who captained Llanelli in the heroic struggle against the Wallabies in 1947, but I got to know him during his time as a highly respected Llanelli committeeman where he always had a word of encouragement for us youngsters.

Byron Gale will always be remembered for two quite remarkable performances for Llanelli, one against the 1967 Wallabies and the other against the 1970 Springboks. Let's be honest, Byron was a tough cookie and he took no prisoners. The front row selected to face Australia was an awesome unit and, in a titanic struggle up front, Glan Morgan, Byron and brother Norman completely overpowered their opponents. It remains a mystery why such a renowned scrummager never partnered his brother in the red jersey of Wales. In one practice session prior to Wales's match against New Zealand in 1967, the West Wales front row opposed their international counterparts. West Wales, captained by Clive Rowlands and coached by Carwyn, were due to play the All Blacks on the Tuesday prior to the international and it should have been a bonding session. 'We're all in this together' was the cry but it became a brutal contest in the front row between Neath second row, Brian Thomas, selected as prop for

Brian Butler was one of the stars of Llanelli's famous one-point defeat at the hands of the 1970 Springboks. Taking the line-out ball here is South Africa's Frik Du Preez. (PA Images)

Wales, and Byron. The Llanelli man took him apart – on one occasion the scrummage erupted and a mass brawl ensued. Byron had that effect on opponents!

Colossal is just one way to describe Brian Butler, a schoolboy contemporary of mine. We were raised a few hundred yards from each other and I'd always bonded with the man probably because we both played together for many years at school, as well as for Felinfoel, Wales Youth and the Scarlets. He always looked after me and believe me at Coleshill School it was comforting to walk the corridors with Brian 'Bull' Butler at your side! He was a record cap holder for the Welsh Youth XV and was in the Coleshill team which defeated Bradford Grammar School in the final of the Llanelli Sevens. I have one abiding memory of him from our days with the national youth team when we faced the England Colts at Beeston. Playing against us that day was the dastardly Nigel Horton who stared at us menacingly during the pre-match reception at the Town Hall and continued his evil deeds on the field of play. He punched Derek Quinnell at the second line-out and, minutes later, floored our skipper Bill Davey, too. Whilst both players were receiving treatment, we came together in a tight huddle and came to an immediate decision. Our hooker, David Dwyer, threw the ball high into the line-out and seconds later Horton lay prostrate on the ground. Brian took care of him and the match which began with a roar ended with a squeak as both teams proceeded to play open, entertaining rugby. We recorded a brilliant victory but the atmosphere in the dressing room afterwards was like a morgue as coach Ieuan Evans objected to our unsavoury tactics. We all spoke our minds, exclaiming, 'If we hadn't retaliated, we'd have been killed!'

Moseley and England's Nigel Horton, an uncompromising opponent when he played against me for England Colts. Brian Butler sorted him out, mind! (PA Images)

Brian soon joined Llanelli and within weeks had become a permanent fixture in our first team. He took his responsibilities in the scrum seriously, making sure that his hooker was well protected. On the other hand, if the opposition had the put-in, then different strategies were employed, not all of them adhering strictly to the law book!

We both played in the first of Wales's two non-cap international matches in Argentina in 1968, but it would be 45 years before the WRU did the decent thing and awarded caps retrospectively for such matches. Be that as it may, it was Brian's performance for Llanelli against South Africa in 1970 which confirmed that he was a player of real promise, so the club was dealt a devastating blow when Bradford Northern announced that the young prop forward had signed professional terms for them. He was one of the hardest prop forwards I ever played with and he would have become a British Lion if he had remained in Wales.

Ken Jones was an employee at Trostre Steel who conscientiously attended night school and as a result became a lecturer in engineering. He showed the same dedication on the field of play and played in Llanelli's front row against the 1951 Springboks. His brother Arthur Jones was equally adept in the front row appearing against the 1947 Wallabies. Ken eventually became club secretary, had his office by the club's reception area and was always available to players and supporters. A hard man and a great man!

Glan Morgan, however, was one of the hardest men ever to don the Llanelli jersey. Vigorous and aggressive, he played against two touring teams: the All Blacks for Swansea in 1963 and versus Australia for the Scarlets in 1967. Then there was Aubrey Gale: a freak! How could an individual play at the top level in the front row, the second row and back row? He was such a versatile forward and in the modern game he would have been in demand as an impact player from the bench, covering all forward positions where his handling skills and uncanny judgement would have attracted club owners and agents alike. Henry

Charles Thomas, father of Imogen, relishes a rumble against Harlequins in 1977, watched by halfbacks Selwyn Williams and David Nicholas. (PA Images)

Morgan was another highly respected prop forward who spent seven years at Stradey Park, representing Wales on two occasions during the 1956–57 season. He made his international debut partnering Ray Prosser and Bryn Meredith in a fearsome front row at the Arms Park against Ireland when the entire Welsh team were ordered off the field by referee Jack Taylor to change their jerseys – he couldn't distinguish between the teams in weather conditions which could only be described as atrocious.

Roy Williams, an international trialist and an outstanding prospect signed for Wigan at the start of the 1952–53 season. It was a cruel blow to the Scarlets who felt that the young forward, who played against the 1951 Springboks, would have been a bastion of their future achievements. Most union players who switched to league were attracted by financial rewards. However, Roy had a specific if somewhat unusual objective. He used the money to finance his training as a solicitor. His son, Peter, was the first to play union for England and league for Wales. Apparently, father Roy (a fluent Welsh speaker and a Plaid Cymru supporter) was delighted when son Peter wore the red jersey for the first time against France in Perpignan.

The Aberporth gaucho, Ricky Evans
(Colorsport/Colin Elsey)

There were others prop forwards who wore that scarlet jersey with pride, like Emrys Evans who played for Cwmgors and Amman United before joining the Scarlets in 1932. Remarkably he was capped at prop forward in 1937 against England before playing against Scotland and Ireland at wing forward. Then there was John Evans from Carmarthen who played against Neil Shehadie's Wallabies and Avril Malan's Springboks, and Tony Crocker from Dafen who will forever be remembered for his role in the win against the All Blacks (he once turned down the opportunity of training with Wales because he was working on a Sunday!). Tony played over 300 games for the Scarlets and was the club's Mr Dependable. His loyalty made him a great clubman and he was the cornerstone of our presence in five consecutive cup finals between 1972 and 1976. Chris Charles contributed immensely to Welsh Cup successes in 1973 and 1974 before signing professional terms for St Helens, whilst Charles Thomas featured for us against Graham Mourie's All Blacks.

(From left) David Young, Ian Watkins, and Llanelli's Anthony Buchanan who formed the Welsh front row against Ireland in 1988. Wales went on to win the Triple Crown.
(Colorsport/Andrew Cowie)

The Gale dynasty continued with Norman's son Sean, who featured on over 200 occasions. Ricky Evans also gave

Deacon Manu on the charge against Leinster.
(Huw Evans Picture Agency)

In the thick of it, Iestyn Thomas. (Huw Evans Picture Agency)

great service, before he was head butted by Olivier Merle at the Parc des Princes in 1995 and, in falling, twisted and broke his leg. Anthony Buchanan's five caps for his country were all gained on foreign soil but he remains a great Scarlet who still gives unstinting service to Llanelli. And what of Deacon Manu, a South Sea Island favourite who gave such wonderful service to the underprivileged in the Llanelli area?

Iestyn Thomas, who won 33 caps for Wales between 2000 and 2007, will be remembered as a great technician whose loyalty to the club held him in high esteem. Iestyn was always in the thick of the action, revelling in scrum, ruck and maul but also contributing in open play with his trademark charges.

John Davies won 34 caps for his country and should have won many more. Interestingly those honours were attained whilst John was with Neath and Richmond. And though he maintained his high standards when he joined Llanelli, he was bizarrely ignored by the Welsh selectors. Along with Brian Williams and Kevin Phillips, John was part of the legendary Gnoll front row of three west Wales farmers, and what he learned at Neath became an integral part of his play. It was commonplace to see John emerge from a mound of bodies and thunder towards the try line clutching the ball safely in his hands.

Other props who were great hits at Llanelli were Spencer John and, of course, Martyn Madden, a cult figure at Stradey Park, where his infectious smile, deceptive bursts and wholeheartedness made him a firm favourite with players and fans. His crucial try against Ebbw Vale in the Welsh cup final at Ashton Gate is still a talking point.

Laurance Delaney was an outstanding scrummager, revered by his peers, even those who did not enjoy the weekly contretemps in the front row as much as Laurance himself. He took his responsibilities in the scrum seriously and was his worth his weight in gold as he could play on both sides of the scrum. I don't think he ever missed a training session during a career which saw him play 501 games for Llanelli and 11 for Wales. His spell in the national team coincided with a difficult period in Welsh rugby when it was suffering from a lack of leadership and direction. Who knows how many caps he would have amassed in another decade? A Dock Stars boy who'd had a tough upbringing, he worshipped the Scarlet jersey. Coming to Stradey Park on a Saturday afternoon was a thrill to him, as was talking to supporters and VIPs – he loved it all and even today he still appreciates what the club has done for him.

Believe me, Barry Llewelyn was something special. We played together as schoolboys and I can vouch for his extraordinary all-round ability. He could play anywhere and he appeared everywhere! He liked to express himself; he was unbelieveably gifted but he was

John 'Cilrhue' Davies plays tractor to Nick Popplewell's trailer at the 1995 Rugby World Cup in a match which Ireland won 24–23. Looking down on proceedings is Derwyn Jones.

(Colorsport/Robert MacFarlane)

Barry Llewelyn (right) was part of Wales's Grand Slam pack of 1971, in the company of the likes of (from left to right) Mervyn Davies, Denzil Williams and Delme Thomas. The English scrum half getting the ball away from this line-out is Jacko Page.

(Colorsport)

Four Scarlets stalwarts celebrate their Schweppes Challenge Cup Final victory over Neath in 1988, (from left) Ieuan Evans, Laurance Delaney, Anthony Buchanan and Phil Davies. Standing behind Phil is another Stradey great, Norman Gale.

(Huw Evans Picture Agency)

also a giant. I remember one training session when Carwyn had invited a local team to provide opposition, and which ended with a 20-minute game which saw New Dock Stars (or Hendy, I'm not quite sure) determined to disrupt. We had been practising Barry's favourite line-out peel that night, and when it came to the game he executed it to perfection and, in true Dalek fashion, exterminated the enemy. He plunged over for the try with five players hanging on for dear life.

His finest hour was against the All Blacks in 1972. It was an epic encounter; a bloody, bruising affair in which Barry displayed qualities which amazed us. As he emerged from the tunnel at Stradey, it was quite obvious that he was up for it, a caged tiger about to be released. And he set about the men in black in no uncertain fashion! If he had made himself available for the 1971 and 1974 Lions, he would have been one of the all-time greats. He, like Laurance Delaney, most certainly plays in Phil Bennett's Greatest Scarlets XV Ever.

1&3 PROPS

Believe me, Barry Llewelyn was something special and here he puts the fear of God into London Welsh, including Gerald Davies, whose right eye and half a moustache we can just make out.

(Colorsport)

Norman Gale leads Wales out at Cardiff against the 1967 All Blacks.
He was an integral part of the Scarlets as player, coach and administrator.

(PA Images)

Chapter 7

2

HOOKER

Hookers are a breed apart. If I had to walk at night along the mean steeets of south Chicago, they are the men I'd like at my side. Tough as teak, they could disfigure masonry!

The hooker's duties, however, have changed immeasurably during the last 25 years – what is expected of a Ken Owens or Emyr Phillips differs greatly from what was so engrained in a Norman Gale or Roy Thomas. And like the special ingredient handed down in an old family recipe, what goes on in the front row is a secret known only to a select few.

In the good old days the main objective was to win the ball in the scrummage on one's own put-in and occasionally strike successfully against the head. It's true to say that some hookers of old would, when asked some five hours after the final whistle who won the match, say 'I've no idea, but I took three strikes against the head!' But over the years hookers striking for the ball became a rarer and rarer sight; it was left to the whole front row to squeeze their opponents into submission and with the aid of the remaining forwards push relentlessly to gain possession. However, the recent law changes mean that hookers have had to strike once more and some find the art a difficult one to master. Since the early 1970s, the hooker has also replaced the wing as the player who throws in the ball at the line-out. Hours of practice are now spent on perfecting the technique – finding your man in the line-out is of paramount importance.

Llanelli and the Scarlets can boast a long line of extremely competent hookers going back to Bryn Evans who represented Wales on six occasions in the 1930s. In 1933, and in front of a record championship crowd of 64,000, which included the Prince of Wales, Evans's first cap brought Wales their historic first win at Twickenham after a 23-year wait. (In this match the International Board's ruling that the first forwards on the spot should be the first forwards down in the scrummage was given a trial. They felt that over-specialisation was harmful to the game. So much for health and safety!)

Scarlets hooker Bryn Evans won his first cap in Wales's victory over Twickenham in 1933. It was a team of Welsh rugby royalty: (back row, l. to r.) Bryn Evans, Viv Jenkins, Wilf Wooller, Iorrie Isaacs, Tom Arthur, B. Thomas, touch judge W.J. Llewelyn; (front row, l. to r.) Arthur Jones, Raymond Jones, Ronnie Boon, Watcyn Thomas, Claude Davey, Edgar Jones, Archie Skym; (on ground, l. to r.) Harry Bowcott, Maurice Turnbull. (PA Images)

Bryn was a revered name in Felinfoel and Llanelli – he was born in 1905 and played for the Welsh Schoolboys, whose contribution to the development of the game in Wales for nigh on a century cannot be underestimated. He was a local hero; people talked about him long after his retirement and although some of the stories might have been slightly exaggerated, I firmly believe that the tales surrounding his immense strength and power were all true because he, like many others, were employed in the heavy industries in the town. How they emerged from such appalling conditions underground, having strained every muscle and sinew, and then produced such stirring performances for club and country, goodness knows.

For many years Roy 'Shunto' Thomas had his own personal debenture seat at the old National Stadium. He was on the replacements bench on twenty or more occasions for Wales, but was recently awarded a cap for the game he played for a Wales XV against Tonga in 1974 in what had been, at the time, billed as a non-capped match. The north Gower was his paradise and as he said, 'I always had the advanatage of looking across the Loughor estuary at my beloved Stradey Park and Llanelli.'

Roy Thomas is most definitely amongst the five top characters I've been privileged to meet during my association with the game: jovial after a win but equally positive and inspirational following a defeat. Roy's philosophy was a simple one: 'Life is meant to be lived'. In the BBC Wales documentary *Who beat the All Blacks,* Roy stole the show with his witty comments and warm, infectious personality. He once told us that Ken Lewis from Penclawdd was the best prop forward he'd ever played with – 'He gave a 22-stone prop from Seven Sisters a torrid time in the scrummages and afterwards drank 45 pints, but was up and around brick laying the following morning!' 'And Phil, Paul Jones (Squat) destroys all props in West Wales rugby!' 'Then why isn't he playing for us or the All Whites?' I quipped. The reply was immediate, 'Phil *bach*, he's too busy. He's cockling in Penclawdd – he hasn't got time!'

I once represented Swansea Police in a charity sevens tournament at St Helen's, competing against local sides Mumbles, Bonymaen, Swansea University and the All Whites. As a result of some animosity between the local constabulary and the university students, I was bombarded with ice cream cornets as I emerged from the tunnel. Roy having delivered coal all day was as black as the ace of spades

'All yours, Selwyn!' With left hand outstretched Roy Thomas shepherds his scrum half at the Richmond Athletic Ground in 1976. (Colorsport/Colin Elsey)

but still appeared in his pristine white kit. During the tour to Hong Kong and Japan in 1975, he had purchased a new set of dentures. They were enormous! And when he tried to say a few words on the bus, the false teeth emerged from his mouth at breakneck speed. After that, he remained toothless throughout the tour!

Roy would have been lost in the modern era. How could he have remained in the Vale of Glamorgan complex without his cockle and laverbread breakfast? He was suited to his own era: a hard and uncompromising forward who would have had to be carried off on a stretcher. He represented Llanelli with pride. I once asked him, 'Who's the best hooker you've ever played against?' His reply was something of a surprise, 'It has to be Morton Howells of Aberavon because he could strike with both feet.' One of his most memorable performances was in a Schweppes Cup match at Pontypool Park in the mid 1970s when the Llanelli forwards completely demolished the Pooler pack on the way to a 24–0 win.

Short, squat, and dynamically quick, David Fox was an athlete who could have played in the centre. He relished Peter Herbert's fitness sessions where he was always in competition with Mark Perego and Iwan Jones. Whilst the majority of the squad were out on their feet during pre-season training at Cefn Sidan, Dai was in his element. He was always first to the top of the dunes and, with others collapsing jelly-legged in heaps, Dai would be pleading for another circuit. Whilst never capped, he was an outstanding forward.

It was always an ambition at Llanelli for non-internationals to represent their club against touring teams – a dream fulfilled by three local hooker-heroes. Graham Jeffreys faced the New Zealand Army in 1945, Australia in 1947 and South Africa in 1951, while Cyril Higgins met the might of the All Blacks in 1953. David Hopkins from Felinfoel had a great temperament and played against Australia in 1957. As a youngster, I remember seeing him play at Stradey and at 6'1" stood out in a fearsome front row. He was a great friend of Ray Williams, and whilst I never heard him talk about rugby, he was a passionate and enthusiastic cricket follower.

The 1970s and early 1980s saw the emergence of four outstanding technicians who never played for Wales but could have done. Meirion Davies, although glued to the bench during the victory against the All Blacks in 1972, played a vital role in our success. Meirion was different from other hookers of his day: a great sevens exponent with skilful hands and a wonderful rugby brain, he was like an extra back-row forward with his pace and guile. Another creative sevens player was Arwyn Reynolds who played his part in a marvellous Llanelli performance against South Africa in 1970, and contributed to the two spectacular tries scored that day by Alan Richards and Brian Butler. Fearless and unflinching, Howard Thomas from Trebannws was a quiet individual whose total commitment and workmanlike performances made him a fine team player, as was evident during his fine all-round performance against Graham Mourie's All Blacks in 1980. Keri Townley was another hooker who was highly respected at Stradey and won plaudits for his handling skills along with his doggedness and tenacity.

It might surprise readers when I state that Matthew Rees – formerly of the Celtic Warriors, now of the Cardiff Blues – is the only Llanelli and Scarlets front-row forward to have represented the club in a Test match for the British Lions. He will always be held in high esteem at Parc y Scarlets: a role model to his peers, his strength of character held him in good stead during his recent battle against cancer which he has now overcome in typical Matthew fashion. Not

A great player and a great man, Matthew Rees.

(PA Images)

only did he survive but within a few months had returned to the Blues starting XV. His performance for the Scarlets in a stunning Heineken Cup match against Ulster at Ravenhill in 2006 typified his strength of character and all-round ability. The match was played in a downpour and, as BBC Wales's rugby correspondent on that never-to-be-forgotten afternoon, I still marvel at the quality of rugby played in such atrocious conditions resulting in a 35–11 win. On the return flight to south Wales that evening everyone was singing the praises of the performance along with the Llanelli hooker's total commitment to the cause.

Matthew Rees shows his total commitment to the cause as he is tackled by Adi Jacobs (left) and Ruan Pienaar during the 2009 Lions series in South Africa.

(PA Images)

I also remember the brutal confrontation between the Lions and the Springboks in 2009. During the first Test match Phil Vickery, the Lions tight-head prop forward, was hung out to dry by the opposition, but undeterred the Welsh front row of Jenkins, Rees and Jones rejuvenated and inspired the Lions in the next Test.

He was a truly inspirational captain for the Scarlets, Wales and now for the Blues: his iron will and single-mindedness has always proved inspirational to younger colleagues. His honesty was always forthcoming in post-match interviews: 'We've lost today. We have no excuses. We just weren't good enough!' Matthew's rugby story reverberated around the rugby world – a great player and a great man!

Andrew Lamerton was a magnificent all-round footballer who deservedly won five caps for his country during the 1993 season. He could play anywhere and I well remember a difficult encounter against the Old Parish at Maesteg where his atheticism and boundless supply of energy inspired the Scarlets to a great win. He played at wing forward that day and exhibited his versatility.

For many seasons Robin McBryde was an ever-present in the middle of the Llanelli front row. He joined the exodus across the Loughor Bridge after a number of seasons with Swansea, and was continually complimented for his committed, robust style of play both nationally and internationally. He represented Wales on 37 occasions and was part of Graham Henry's British and Irish Lions squad in Australia in 2001. Robin was as hard as nails, never afraid to take on an adversary, big or small. I still remember vividly an unsavoury incident in north Gwent in the 1990s where terrible conditions and negligible visibility were making life difficult for referee and players alike, and the Llanelli hooker nowhere near the ball was taken out illegally by one of the opposition. To be honest, I cringed at the

sight of the incident and with Robin doubled up in pain, it seemed inevitable that he was on his way to the local A&E department. If the incident had been seen by the referee, it would have been an immediate sending off. However, the recipient of *The Strongest Man* title on television, obviously in immense pain, just got up and carried on playing! Off the field, Robin is modest and extremely affable, and is now a much respected coach at the highest level.

Two under Robin's charge at national level are current Scarlets hookers Ken Owens and Emyr Phillips. Ken has been in Richard

Hibbard's shadow for a while but now seems destined to step into the limelight and make the position his own in the national team. A Carmarthenshire lad, Ken will never ignore you and if he ever decides to stand for county council election would most certainly top the poll! He is a born leader who brings a different tempo to the side with his blistering pace and splendid technique. He exemplifies the Llanelli spirit in all aspects of play.

The thin red line. Andrew Lamerton steps in at scrum half against Australia at Stradey in 1992, shielded by (from left to right) Phil Davies, Ricky Evans, Rupert Moon, Mark Perego (obscured), Tony Copsey and Laurance Delaney.

(Colorsport)

A well-known supermarket chain has its *Finest* range – exceptional produce often stacked on a special shelf. And it is in

Wales's strongest man, Robin McBryde keeps the ball away from Leicester Tigers in 1996.

(PA Images)

the Scarlets *Finest* domain that Norman Gale will remain until my dying day. In his younger days he came up against the mighty Bryn Meredith from Newport who distinguished himself on the Lions tours of 1955, 1959 and 1962. It was a huge coup for the Scarlets when Gorseinon born and bred Gale joined the club from Swansea in 1961. He was first capped whilst at the All Whites in 1960, replacing the injured Meredith, and went on to win a further 24 caps between 1963 and 1969, captaining his country against New Zealand in 1967 and England at Twickenham in 1968. Norman was at home at Stradey Park, the ground unkempt perhaps but it had that working class feel about it which made the players feel at home.

Emyr Phillips handles like a centre against Connacht.

(Huw Evans Picture Agency)

Norman relished the physical side of the sport. There may not have been outright war in the dark depths of the scrum, but there were ceratinly battles going on which had no relation to the game itself. In all aspects Norman could stand his ground and more often than not could come away victorious. To secure the championship in 1968 (my very first full season), we had to win the last match of the season against Neath. How times have changed! It was an evening kick-off with players parking on side streets before walking the quarter mile or so to the Gnoll. There was an undercurrent of bad feeling between the two teams which had carried over from previous encounters. However, Norman, who was the club captain, took me aside prior to kick off and assured me that he would be at my side throughout the eighty minutes. I had been suffering from a pain in the right groin but Norman's plea could not be ignored – 'You have to play on one leg!' Despite losing Alan John in the first half with a broken collarbone and being reduced to 13 men for a period when Marlston Morgan broke his nose, we defended relentlessly and won a dour affair by 9–0. Dennis Thomas was injured but Gareth Thomas came into the side and caused all sorts of problems with his deft kicking and intelligent probing. A Marlston Morgan try, a Norman Gale penalty goal and a dropped goal by yours truly brought the spoils back to Stradey Park. The smiles on the faces of the supporters were a joy to behold but there was little time for celebrating as we all had to be at work the following morning.

Great credit has to be given to chairman Peter Rees for his vision and decision making for it was he who brought fitness guru Tom Hudson to the club, and what an impression he made during our success in the 1970s! Tom and Norman were on the same wavelength and Llanelli as a club made huge strides under their leadership. There

There must be a way through, thinks Ken Owens as he drives on against Clermont.

(Niall Carson/PA Wire)

were two sides to Norman – the tough, streetwise front-row forward and the intelligent rugby brain, who knew that in a rugby match only one team can win! He certainly hadn't been born to be a loser.

Another cameo comes to mind when I think of Norman. Old Deer Park was packed to the rafters for the Llanelli v London Welsh encounter in 1967. John Dawes's team was packed with raw talent and to be fair we too had our share of players who could change the course of a match in an instant with some scintillating play. However, Norman as captain had other thoughts. 'We're going to take this lot up front. Phil, it's limited rugby this afternoon.' The purists were disappointed; the technical perfection and breathtaking running usually associated with both sides was missing as the Scarlets won a dull contest 15–8.

I played with some great hookers and he stands with Peter Wheeler and Bobby Windsor as the best. His team talks were quite frightening on occasions and certainly motivated us prior to leaving the dressing room. I had so much admiration for the man who should have represented the British and Irish Lions in New Zealand in 1966 and South Africa in 1968 – he was quite simply one of the best hookers in world rugby at the time but was unfairly overlooked. I wonder what would have happened if he had captained the Lions on those two occasions? As a spectator I saw Norman in action for Wales against New Zealand in Auckland in 1969. Wales were well beaten but Norman Reginald Gale led the charge. The likes of Meads and Gray held no fears for him. He stood up to them and I well remember a Barry John up-and-under in the second half with two men in eager pursuit – Mervyn Davies and Norman Gale. He was a credit to Wales. He was an incredible man and was an integral part of Llanelli Rugby Football Club as player, captain, coach, chairman and president. He is my hooker in the Greatest Scarlets XV Ever.

Standing alone, the incredible Norman Gale.
(Colorsport)

Delme Thomas, an immense presence for club, country and the Lions.
(Colorsport)

Chapter 8

4 & 5
THE SECOND ROW

Rugby has always claimed to be a game for everyone, offering a place in the team for all shapes and sizes, accommodating the tall and the short, the fat and the thin, with democratic zeal. There is even room for the giant, and that room is the team's engine room, the second row.

To some followers, it is the open-field running of the backs which generates the most excitement. However, for the purist it is the hard graft of the forwards which captures the true essence of the game, and second-row forwards have always been, to a man, grafters. These locks (as they are now called) are the powerhouses of any pack, but they can be as dynamic and dextrous as the silkiest threequarter. Indeed to see big men soaring above everyone in the line-out and plucking

R.H. Williams: 'You could build a maul around him'.

(PA Images)

Colin Meads, chairman of the R.H. Williams fan club, looks to pass against the Barbarians in 1964. Behind him is another great second row, Brian Price.

(PA Images)

the ball out of the sky stirs as much passion as seeing a centre sidestep his man. And the Scarlets have had more than their fair share of second-row forwards who have combined the grunt and the grace.

Llanelli, Wales and Lions supporters of the 1950s will never forget R.H. 'Rhys' Williams, the human dynamo with the distinctive red hair who put the fear of God into all who opposed him. As a youngster on the Tanner Bank at Stradey, I was overcome by his size. His mere presence commanded respect and although he came up against some of the truly great forwards of his day he was never intimidated and always seemed to produce the goods. But don't take my word for it. Ask a man who knows. Which is what I did at a recent dinner in London.

Sir Colin Meads of King Country, New Zealand, was one of the greatest rugby players of all time. I'd got to know him reasonably well since our first meeting back in 1969 and as the evening progressed I casually asked him, 'Well, Sir Colin – how good was R.H. Williams?' His reply was immediate. 'He was one of the hardest, toughest men I ever played against. He was so strong – you could build a maul around him. A remarkable player; one of the greatest players I played against.' I was dumbfounded – this was the RH whom I'd hero worshipped and who was born and bred in the anthracite-mining village of Cwmllynfell on the slopes of the Black Mountain.

The evening's Master of Ceremonies was the likeable Martin Bayfield, the 6' 10" lock who'd represented England and the Lions in the 1990s, but is more famous, perhaps, for playing Robbie Coltrane's double as the half giant Hagrid in the Harry Potter films. Colin had never met him before. 'How would you have coped with him?' I enquired. 'Simple, really Phil' said the great man, 'I would have broken his ribs in the second line-out!'

Stan Williams was a big, muscular man who won six caps for his country in the late 1940s. I had the privilege of working with him at Llanelli Steelworks where his quiet disposition and engaging personality created quite an impression. He never talked about his rugby career and sadly died at a relatively young age after serving Llanelli as a hardworking committeeman (he was pressed into service against Newport at Stradey Park in 1955 at the age of 40). Frederick Luther Morgan from Pontyberem played for four seasons at Stradey Park and was the first pupil from Gwendraeth Grammar School to gain international honours. His career was interrupted by the Second World War and played his last game of rugby at the age of 24. Des Jones from Tumble joined from Aberavon in 1947 and will always be remembered as a try scorer against Basil Kenyon's 1951 Springboks, being in the right place at the right time after a snaking Lewis Jones run. Des's solitary international appearance was against England at Twickenham in 1949 in a 3–3 draw.

Martin Bayfield, Lions second row and half giant! (PA Images)

Gethin Hughes, although never capped, appeared in innumerable Welsh trials and was the backbone of the club in the early 1950s partnering R.H. Williams in the 17–3 defeat against New Zealand in 1953. It was a gallant performance but eventually the All Blacks took control scoring 11 points after the Scarlets had lost left wing Ron Thomas through injury. After him, Keith Rowlands came to prominence having joined from London Welsh in the late 1950s to

Keith Rowlands disrupts Ireland's Willie John McBride in the Dublin mud of 1963. (PA Images)

A force to be reckoned with, Stuart Gallacher shields the ball from London Welsh's headbanded Mervyn Davies at Old Deer Park in 1969. (Colorsport/Colin Elsey)

form a powerful second-row combination with RH. He marked his first cap in 1962 with a gutsy, all-round display at the Arms Park against France which resulted in a Lions tour place to South Africa. He played in three of the four test matches scoring a try in the fourth test at Bloemfontein.

I was aware of Stuart Gallacher's potential from an early age as we played together for Felinfoel Youth where he demonstrated his natural ability as a line-out forward and all-round footballer. He was a presence at set pieces but was also a force to be reckoned with in open play, and had the privilege of captaining Llanelli against South Africa in 1970 in one of the great Scarlet performances. Though they lost by a point, they matched the visitors try for try, including one spectacular score which saw eighteen home players handle before Alan Richards plunged over in the right-hand corner. It was a huge blow when the club lost Stuart and Brian Butler to rugby league, but at least Stuart departed having contributed to Wales's win against France at the National Stadium in 1970, when his chargedown led to Dai Morris's crucial try in a 11–6 victory.

I grew up with Derek Quinnell. We were in the same class at Coleshill Secondary Modern School. He was Llanelli through and through, who made himself into a tough man, a respected adversary who could never be underestimated. Derek would be the first to admit that training was not his favourite pastime. He was always late for Tom Hudson's sessions and although there were rumblings of disciplinary action it never materialised because we wanted Derek in our line-up for important fixtures. He was always the first name on the team sheet because Derek Quinnell was the real deal, a truly outstanding player. There was one incident when DQ arrived late for a training session. Several selectors wanted to omit him from the team. As captain I immediately retaliated – 'If Derek isn't playing I'm out of here!' Derek played.

He was also versatile, as he proved on that fine, cool afternoon at Wellington in 1971. Surprisingly, DQ had been chosen for the third Lions Test at blind-side wing forward to combat the threat of Sid Going and the volatile Alex Wyllie. Both were reduced to bit part players. It had been many a year since an All Black team had suffered so badly in the contest for the ball.

Derek Quinnell's finest hour, however, had to be that match at Stradey Park in October 1972. But there were many other red-

The beautiful game! Second-row partners Phil May (left) and Derek Quinnell keep the 1975 Wallabies at bay at Stradey.
(Colorsport/Colin Elsey)

letter days. Did not Cliff Morgan breathlessly exclaim 'Brilliant by Quinnell!' as Derek put Gareth away for that much-replayed try for the Barbarians in 1973? Derek always strove for perfection and gave his all as much to satisfy himself as to please others.

Phil May. What a player! What a servant! He played over 500 games for the club and proved himself an inspirational leader of men. I can still visualise him at the front of a line-out, brushing the opposition aside and claiming possession with a minimum of effort. At a packed Sardis Road on a Wednesday evening in the early 1990s, Pontypridd under Mike Watkins's leadership, were all pumped up and ready 'to kick ***t' out of the visiting Scarlets. I was working for BBC radio and felt rather uneasy as both teams took the field. They'd obviously targeted Phil and Laurance Delaney but both men put their bodies on the line and withstood the early Ponty onslaught. They were the two men the home team had to nullify if they were to win but both men never gave less than their all and inspired the Scarlets to an

The likeable rogue, Chris Wyatt, leaps highest against Leinster.

(Huw Evans Picture Agency)

excellent victory. It was a marvellous moment when Phil was selected for Wales for the very first time at the grand old age of 31. To be honest his omission had been a mystery to us all. His debut was at Twickenham when two Adrian Hadley tries proved decisive in a 11–3 victory. 'Great' is an often used word in rugby football but Phil May was a Stradey great!

I don't think Llanelli supporters realised how good a player Phil Davies was! He set himself one of the hardest training programmes I have ever come across and was more than willing to go that extra mile. Whilst others lazed in the summer months, Phil took up athletics with Terry Davies and Paul Oram at Stebonheath and worked his socks off to improve his running technique. Born and bred in the mining village of Seven Sisters, his love for the game had been engrained at an early age and it was no surprise that his all-round footballing ability made him an ever-present for Llanelli and Wales for a decade or more. Muscular and explosive, he was an excellent front-of-the-line jumper and showed his versatility by appearing in the second and back row for club and country. I have no hesitation in stating that Phil was a truly outstanding Scarlet.

Mike Voyle gave great service to the Scarlets as did second rows of earlier vintage, like Russell Cornelius from Pyle, Elwyn Jenkins from Cwmgwili (who later became a Methodist minister), Bryan Thomas, who captained the team in the early 1960s, Robert Fouracre, Roger Powell, who played in an England trial, the combative Rhys Thomas and the loyal Hywel Rees.

Chris Wyatt must rank as one of the best footballing second-row forwards I've seen.

This man could run as fast as a back-row forward and possessed hands which could have graced the Chicago Bulls. To be perfectly honest he didn't lack for anything on the pitch, but Chris enjoyed the social side of rugby football which meant that he wasn't quite as committed to fitness and conditioning as some of his other teammates. In essence he was a likeable rogue who could have been a British Lion.

Can you believe that a Cockney crossed the Loughor Bridge and immersed himself totally in the Llanelli culture? Tony Copsey was a very intelligent guy, at work with Camford Plastics and at play with Llanelli RFC. His years spent in the area meant that he qualified residentially and therefore attracted the attention of the national selectors. However, his first cap out in Lansdowne Road should have resulted in a red card after a haymaker on Neil Francis but amazingly he got away with it as the officials were unsighted at the time. He was a rugged forward who took no prisoners when the going got tough.

For all his superhuman qualities on the field, Delme Thomas was the gentlest, most reliable and highly thought of person off it. He was taught by Howard 'Ash' Davies at St Clears Secondary School

'You could trust Delme when we went into battle...' JPR (extreme left) and I look on as Delme Thomas knows only one way against the 1972 All Blacks at Cardiff.

(PA Images)

and eventually the athletically built second-row forward from Bancyfelin was capped at youth level. It proved a meteoric rise to fame and for the next twenty years he faithfully made the 20-mile journey from his home village to Stradey Park to play for his beloved Scarlets. There was always an aura about him. When I joined Llanelli, Delme was already an established figure having played in Test matches for the British Lions in New Zealand before winning his first Welsh cap against Australia in 1966. He was always quiet and dignified and revelled in encouraging new arrivals at the club. Physically he was a giant of a man with powerful, muscular arms which he used to good effect in the line-out where he was able to outmanoeuvre the opposition by clean catching or deft tap-downs. He was a super scrummager and immense in rucks and mauls.

He partnered Willie John McBride in three Lions tours in 1966, 1968 and 1971. 'You could trust Delme when we went into battle,' remarked the Ulsterman, 'and all who played with him can testify to his commitment, ability and total dedication to the cause.' His wonderful speech to us players prior to the All Blacks match at Stradey in 1972 will live with me for ever. You could have heard a pin drop:

> I've worn the Lions jersey in Test matches. I was part of the Lions squad which returned victorious from New Zealand in 1971. I was a Grand Slam winner with Wales in 1971 and I was proud to wear the Barbarian jersey on numerous occasions… I'm prepared to give it all away for a victory this afternoon.

Jake Ball, the scarlet-bearded, Ascot-born, Aussie-raised, Welsh international lock drives into Ospreys' Rhys Webb. Jake and South African George Earle have forged a formidable partnership in the second row.

(Huw Evans Picture Agency)

It was an emotional oration, but the captain didn't raise his voice. There was no bad language. It was uttered to men from his hinterland. It was short and to the point and left grown men crying. And to Grav, *'Cofia Ray, ma' dy dad 'da ti fan hyn prynhawn 'ma!'* ('Remember, Ray, your dad is here with you this afternoon!') The All Blacks had been defeated prior to kick-off.

Delme Thomas retired in 1974 but came out of retirement in 1975 when we were forced to play two matches on the same afternoon – a Schweppes Cup match away to Amman United and a normal friendly fixture at Rodney Parade. We sent our best XV to Cwmaman and as we trouped off the field after winning 51–0, a number of the opposition were heard to boast, 'I've played against Delme!' That says it all!

I don't think any one will argue with me as to who the two best second-row forwards to represent the Scarlets are. R.H. Williams and Delme Thomas are shoo-ins. Just ask Colin Meads and Amman United!

Delme Thomas, muscular arm outstretched, is determined to lay his hand on the ball (or at least on Willie John's face!) at Cardiff in 1973.

(Colorsport)

An awesome talent, Scott Quinnell defying gravity against Leicester in the 2002 European Cup semi-final at Nottingham.

(Colorsport/Matthew Impey)

Chapter 9

8 Number Eight

For most young rugby players, the ultimate dream is to play at outside half. This is the glamour position, but as these young players grow in stature and experience then another position catches the eye, one which is equally challenging and vital to the way the team plays, that of the no. 8. The present role model in the position is the Argentine-born Sergio Parisse, who plays in the Championnat for Stade Français and at international level for Italy. How he manages to put in rousing performances in a side which loses most of its games is testament to the talent and commitment of the player. Imagine what he could do in a winning side!

We too in Wales have produced world-class no. 8 forwards, Alun Pask, for instance. I'll never forget the match between Wales and France at the Arms Park in 1962, when wing three-quarter Henri Rancoule was eating up the turf on his way to the try line. Hot on his

Italian superhero no. 8, Sergio Parisse
(PA Images)

heels was Alun Pask. With everyone in the stadium on their feet in anticipation, the French flyer was brought down short by a last ditch tackle by the man from Abertillery. The cheering from the fans could be heard as far as Llandaff and Gabalfa!

During the 1970s, however, it was Mervyn Davies who dominated this position for club, country and the British Lions. Tall and gangly with his trademark spaghetti western moustache, he appeared cumbersome as he strolled onto the field-of-play but once the referee blew his whistle he was transformed into an all-action hero and a natural leader. The respect shown to Mervyn from players from all over the globe was testament to his ability as a truly magnificent no 8.

It would be an easy matter to write a whole chapter on the accomplishments of Watcyn Thomas. Educated at Llanelli County School, he became the first captain of the Welsh Secondary Schools XV in 1924. He enjoyed enormous success playing at second row and no. 8 for Llanelli, Swansea, Waterloo and Wales, and his first-class career spanned a decade or more. Talented and influential, he was a strict disciplinarian and never afraid to take risks and to make snap

Another of Wales's world-class no. 8 forwards, Alun Pask dives over at Twickenham in 1966.
(PA Images)

decisions when the situation demanded a change of tactics. Against Scotland in 1931, the Welsh pack was having a torrid time in the scrummage but in a moment of pure inspiration (or maybe desperation) Thomas as pack leader decided to switch prop Tom Day to play hooker – this changed the course of the game and led to a Welsh victory. Incidentally Thomas fractured his clavicle but refused to leave the field and scored a vital try.

Watcyn Thomas was the captain when Wales defeated England for the first time at Twickenham in 1933. As the main jumper in the line-out, he would skilfully catch the ball in two hands and in one fluid movement transfer to his scrum half. Knowing full well that his forwards understood Welsh, Thomas decided to utilise this to their advantage by shouting out his calls in their native tongue. Unbeknown to him, one of the England back-row forwards, Lieutenant Vaughan Jones, originally from Pontarddulais, was a fluent Welsh speaker and so the advantage was soon neutralised!

Watcyn's last Welsh international match was played at Ravenhill, Belfast in 1933. The Welsh selectors had caused a sensation by choosing to play Bob Barrell, the Cardiff prop, at back-row forward and Arthur Lemon, the Neath flanker, in the front row. Thomas, as captain, was having none of it and so the players reverted to their preferred positions as soon as the national anthems were sung. It proved to be Watcyn Thomas's swansong!

Born and bred in Garnant in the Amman valley, Jim Lang was a tinplate worker (of Himalayan height according to Dai Smith and Gareth Williams in *Fields of Praise*) who played a total of 12 international games for his country including the memorable match against New

All-action hero and natural leader, Mervyn Davies.

(Colorsport/Colin Elsey)

Zealand in 1935 where his domination of the line-out proved crucial in Wales's 13–12 victory. His first game for Llanelli was in March 1929 when the gateman refused to accept that he was a Llanelli player and as a result Lang had to pay a shilling to get into the ground!

Emyr Lewis, 'Tarw' ('the Bull'), to his contemporaries, was one of the finest young talents I saw at Stradey Park. He joined the club as a raw police cadet and became an instant hero following a rousing performance against Swansea when he single-handedly took the All Whites apart. From a scrummage on the Swansea 22-metre line, Emyr picked the ball up and ran at the opposition. The determination in his face was evident as he scattered the defence with legs pumping menacingly. There were no sidesteps, no swerves – he just blazed his way to the try line with two would-be tacklers clinging on hopefully to his muscular frame. It was a statement to players, supporters and selectors alike. The place erupted.

Emyr Lewis, the Bull, scattering the Cardiff defence in 1993. (Huw Evans Picture Agency)

Emyr never drew inspiration from a captain's pre-match team talk. Just putting on his kit was enough motivation and once on the field he could be seen charging around after his opponents. But even today, some twenty years following his international retirement, the Welsh rugby public still talk about how Emyr deftly delivered a kick which bisected England's defending three-quarters and provided half a chance for Ieuan Evans who gave chase. Evans left Rory Underwood in his wake as he managed to get boot to ball. The rest is history as the Scarlet express controlled the ball and claimed a match-winning score, thus depriving England of a third consecutive Grand Slam.

Emyr's time at Llanelli coincided with the arrival of another impressive no. 8, and soon Tarw had to relinquish his favoured position at club and international level to Scott Quinnell. Emyr's 41 caps for Wales speaks volumes for his ability, however, and I'm convinced that if the game had been fully

One that got away: Ben Morgan came on in leaps and bounds at the Scarlets, as he shows here against Northampton

(Huw Evans Picture Agency)

professional in the early 1990s, then Emyr Lewis would have been a British and Irish Lion.

Ben Morgan was sent to Parc y Scarlets on the recommendation of Merthyr's Peter Morgan. 'I know he's unfit and overweight but there's something about him which suggests he could become an international rugby player.' And thanks to the training regime at the club, Ben worked his socks off and developed into an outstanding ball carrier, not the fastest over 50 metres but dynamic and explosive over ten. He was an extremely polite young man who had dual qualifications, but the man from Dursley on the Severn estuary always favoured England and it was no surprise when he worked his way into Stuart Lancaster's international squad. His performance in the first Test in New Zealand in 2014 was world class and summed up by his pick-up and 25-metre run from a scrummage on his own goal line when the men in black were cast aside with utter contempt.

Over a period of 11 seasons and 404 games, Hefin Jenkins was an ever-present for Llanelli, having first appeared for us in 1969 against Swansea at Stradey Park. Unfortunately he played in the same era as Mervyn Davies, the world's foremost no. 8 forward at the time, which meant he never played for Wales. On the one occasion when Mervyn was sidelined through injury, fate dealt Hefin a cruel blow as he too, with an ankle injury, was incapacitated. In the latter part of his career he suffered from various ailments, which allowed Jeff Squire and Derek Quinnell to come to the fore in Wales's back row. We often marvelled at Hefin's all-round skills, including a neat dummy and feint, all of which made him a quite outstanding seven-a-side player.

He was a force to be reckoned with in Llanelli's marvellous cup triumphs in the 1970s and his performances for the club against South Africa in 1970 and New Zealand in 1972 were remarkable. Off the field Hefin was a lovely man, a gentleman who, whatever the

Hefin Jenkins comes up for air in the open field against Richmond.
(Colorsport)

circumstances, had a smile on his face. But once he donned the scarlet jersey, he changed into a hard, physical presence who could cause chaos from the base of the scrum as well as dominating the back of the line-out. Since his retirement as a player Hefin served the club with distinction and his recent passing away was a blow to us all.

Marlston Morgan's career and mine overlapped briefly towards the end of the 1960s, when I witnessed first hand his love for the game. He was ready for action as soon as he put on his jersey and once on the field exhibited qualities which made him a pleasure to play with and a brute to play against. Rugby union football was a collision sport as far as Marlston was concerned – he charged around after his opponents, making stomach-curdling tackles and generally making a nuisance of himself. Within milliseconds of flooring his opponent, Marlston was on his feet creating effective platforms from which his fellow players could create attacking moves.

He was not the greatest footballer but he was a real bulldog, as tough as any player I played with or against. His career had progressed from Burry Port to Neath and onwards to Llanelli where he immediately gained the respect of players and supporters alike. His philosophy was a simple one, 'Follow me into the trenches!' In today's professional game where tackle counts impress coaches, Marlston would have been a fixture at blind-side wing forward although his never-say-die attitude should have been rewarded with Welsh caps in the mid-1960s. In one final Welsh trial, fourteen of the Probables were selected for international duty, but disappointingly there was no room for Marlston.

In a championship decider at the Gnoll in 1968, Marlston's face was a mess after he broke his nose in a shattering collision. His eyes were half closed, he was a virtual passenger but he refused to go off – an act which inspired his teammates to battle on for victory. His parents were responsible for the laundry at Stradey Park and it was always a delight to see his mother bringing back the kit in pristine condition. Marlston to this day is a great servant to the club.

Steelworker Ossie Wiliams, a former pupil of my old academy at Coleshill, played for Furnace before embarking on his war service with the Welsh Guards. He played across the back row and was known for his immense strength along with his dribbling prowess. He played seven times for Wales and kicked a penalty goal in an often violent match (played in Arctic conditions) against France at St Helen's in 1948. The French wing three-quarter Michel Pomathios from Agen was the star performer and was chaired off the field by the Welsh fans.

adidas

Go, Scotty! Scott Quinnell leads the Lions charge against Australia at Melbourne in 2001.

(Colorsport/ Simon Baker/Pro Sport [NZ])

World-Cup winning no. 8, David Lyons, a dedicated Scarlet.

(Huw Evans Picture Agency)

It could be said that David Lyons had his best years behind him when he joined the Scarlets in 2008 but it has to said that he dedicated himself to the club and deserves great credit for his loyalty and commitment. In 2004 he was awarded the John Eales medal as the Wallabies player of the year, a year after he had been Australia's no. 8 on that fateful day at Sydney in November 2003 when Jonny Wilkinson's dropped goal won the World Cup for England during extra time. During his first season at Parc y Scarlets, he played every match and captained the club during season 2010–11. David was instrumental in getting his team over the gain line and will be remembered as a real presence at no. 8 whose bravery and vision made him a force to be reckoned with.

Scott Quinnell was a very special talent and I remember saying just that after watching him play schoolboy rugby. He was always a target – after all his father was Derek, his uncle the inimitable Barry John and his godfather the peerless Mervyn Davies! He learnt to look after himself. Like his father he wasn't the greatest fan of the training sessions and felt that 5 x 50m sprints (rather than the de rigeur 10 x 50m) would be sufficient after a tiring match the previous weekend. He would eventually complete the required set but was constantly complaining! Thankfully the coaching staff realised this and made every effort to nurse him through the sessions.

Scott spent a short time at Wigan Rugby League Club which saw him develop into a very useful ball carrier who was used to soften up the opposition. He won the total respect of Wigan followers and possibly played his best rugby at the club. At Central Park he came to realise that you have to win trophies to be considered great. He returned to Stradey when the union game turned professional and his riproaring performances in the scarlet jersey were a source of delight to the vociferous supporters who revelled in his charging, high-octane runs. There was no finer sight on the field than seeing Scott Quinnell breaking from a scrum, decimating the opposing defence, twisting and turning and more often than not ploughing over the try line. His try for Wales against France in 1994 was extraordinary. From a line-out he picked up the ball by his bootlaces, flattened three Frenchmen and then stormed along the touchline to claim the try.

I well remember a Heineken Cup match against Leicester at Stradey Park in 1996 when Scott instantly made his presence felt. Llanelli's kick-off was pefectly lofted and directed towards the

Leicester captain, Martin Johnson. As he took possession, Scott dumped him on his backside – the gargantuan second-row forward had been hurt and was obviously livid that he'd been upended in the opening seconds of the match. It was 1–0 to Llanelli; it exemplified the Scarlets's spirit throughout the contest and even the fanatical Leicester contingent admitted that the incident had defined the game which Llanelli won 34–17. Scott played his final few seasons with knees that were all but wrecked but his leadership qualities and charismatic personality ensured that he will always remain a true great in Llanelli's history – an awesome talent. What is more, he is my choice as Scarlets all-time best no. 8.

4 Aussies v 1 Scarlet: no contest! Lions no. 8 Scott Quinnell scatters all and sundry at Melbourne.

(Colorsport/Matthew Impey)

Derek Quinnell, an exceptional rugby player.

(Colorsport)

Chapter 10

6 & 7 Wing forwards

I never tired of listening to my father and his colleagues singing the praises of Llanelli greats. They were always obsessed with the back row specialists of their day, and endlessly debated the respective merits of those whose duties combined the creative and destructive sides of the game, the open acres and the blind alleys!

Len Davies, elder brother of full-back Terry, was a local boy from Bynea, who won three caps in the mid-1950s. Even though I was only a young boy at the time, I was poignantly aware of the sadness at Stradey when Len, in his mid-twenties, was taken ill and eventually died of leukaemia in 1956.

Hagan Evans was another who impressed and in 1946 scored five tries against London Welsh at Herne Hill. He signed professional terms for Bradford Northern at the start of the 1946–47 season and ended up on the winning team against Leeds in the 1947 Challenge

Josh Turnbull developed into a wing forward of international quality at Parc y Scarlets. Here he secures possession against the Newport Gwent Dragons.

(Huw Evans Picture Agency)

Cup Final at Wembley. In 1953 Hagan's brother, Peter, captained Llanelli against New Zealand and won two caps against England and France in 1951. Their father, Gil Evans, was a senior foreman at Llanelli Steelworks – he was small in stature but an extremely influential character. He looked after me when I started working at the complex making sure I was well away from the heat of the furnaces on match days!

Peter Stone joined the Scarlets from Loughor after resuming studies at Aberystwyth University after the Second World War. A pupil at the legendary Gowerton Grammar School, he faced the 1947 Wallabies and 1951 Springboks, gaining his only cap against France in Paris in March 1949. Ian McGregor was a proud Scotsman who played for the Scarlets whilst stationed at RAF Pembrey. He was a hard-tackling wing forward whose strength and speed around the field coupled with his stamina made him a formidable opponent.

The transition from scrum half to back-row forward is not a normal career progression in rugby football. But such were Clive John's qualities that he was perfectly at home in both positions. A ghost-like runner, like his brother Barry, and an instinctive try scorer, he was possibly the most gifted of all the Johns. His style of play is what the modern player aspires to and his ability to change the tempo of a movement in an instant led to opportunities for others. The journalist Frank Keating once used the words 'double-declutching six times in four strides' to describe rugby league's Brett Kenny. But Clive John was doing all that twenty years before the Paramatta and Wigan legend.

I well remember Clive captaining us in a closely contested match in front of a packed house at Stradey against Bridgend. He got the ball near his own posts and immediately decided to counter-attack rather than clear to touch. He lost possession resulting in an unnecessary Bridgend score. At half time with the players in a huddle, he bravely admitted, 'I made a mistake. I'll make up for it.' And he did! He worked himself into a frenzy in the second period; he was a man inspired, scoring and creating tries.

His other brother Alan, a tearaway open-side wing forward was the complete opposite of the modern player. He was also a Stradey regular whose guts, spirit and abrasive qualities were recognised throughout the Welsh rugby scene. Outside halves never liked playing against him because he stopped you going on the outside – I always wanted to be on his side during practice matches. Alan was also a social animal who enjoyed his pint – even before a match!

Camaraderie! All Black wing Grant Batty invites Barbarians flanker Tommy David to kiss his fist at Cardiff in 1973.

(Colorsport)

Carwyn James wasn't only a coach on the training field; he wanted to improve the club's standing in the rugby community, and as such was always scouting for fresh talent in west Wales and further afield. As a result of impressing for Crawshay's XV in a charity game, Tom David was invited along to see Llanelli play against the Barbarians in September 1972. Soon after he decided to leave Pontypridd and embark on a career with Llanelli which eventually saw him winning international honours and selection for the 1974 British Lions. At his peak he was an immensely strong and effective ball carrier who ran powerfully at outside halves. He only stayed at Stradey Park for three seasons but became part of Carwyn's talented jigsaw in the back row.

He will forever be remembered for the part he played in 'that try' when the Barbarians defeated the All Blacks in January 1973, along with his confrontations that day with wing three-quarter Grant Batty. Tommy returned to Pontypridd who, under his direction became a force in Welsh rugby. Thanks to the paper-thin partitions between the dressing rooms at Sardis Road, it was quite hysterical listening to his team talks – his words obviously inspired Ponty but also provided interesting information for us on their intentions and style of play.

Tom David's transfer to the Scarlets was a body blow for Alan James from Furnace whose ambition throughout his teens was to represent his local town team. This he did splendidly for many seasons but even today he remains devastated that he didn't feature for Llanelli against the 1972 All Blacks. The decision to omit him from the team for the match hurt; being part of the squad and sitting on the bench was scant compensation as he desperately wanted to be on the field of play. During the ecstatic celebrations following our New Zealand victory, club secretary Ken Jones shook Alan and Selwyn by the hand and uttered just the one word, 'Tough!'

I suppose Alan could have returned to play for Furnace before turning out, say, in the black of Neath or the white of Swansea, but the Llanelli jersey meant everything to Alan James: he played with an honesty and an intensity which would have been alien to players who joined from other clubs. His total commitment to the cause even earned him a Welsh trial after one magnificent performance against

Cardiff. He played in the 1972, 1975 and 1976 Schweppes Cup finals for the Scarlets and was prominent in the exciting 28–28 draw with the 1975 Australian tourists. He also remained loyal to the club after his playing days were over, becoming a reliable committeeman and hardworking team manager.

A young, fresh faced David Pickering appeared in 1979 and I had the privilege of playing with him during my last seasons for the club, when he impressed with his pace, ball-handling skills and general all-round ability. Paul Ringer, however, adopted a more old-fashioned approach, flying out from set pieces to manhandle outside halves and take no prisoners. Alun Davies, another rugged back-row forward, was at his peak during season 1980–81 but unfortunately won just one cap, against the 1984 Australian tourists. American David Hodges was a truly outstanding ball handler, having played basketball in his younger days, and gave his all to the club, as did Gary Jones from Pontypridd, an aggressive, feisty flanker who covered every blade of grass. Over the last twenty years Gwyn Jones, Dafydd Jones, Alix Popham and Gavin Thomas carried on the tradition: all four were capped, as was Josh Turnbull, before he turned to greener pastures at Cardiff.

Head down and go! David Pickering has fellow Scarlet Phil Davies on his left as he steams ahead against England at Cardiff in 1985.

(Colorsport)

During the early 1990s, Llanelli were one of the outstanding club sides in European rugby. Indeed the 1992–93 season saw them achieve a league and cup double as well as defeating the world champions Australia in a magnificent match at Stradey Park. The team, superbly coached by Gareth Jenkins and Allan Lewis, played a style of rugby which thrilled spectators far and wide – a brand reminiscent of that witnessed in the 1990s under Carwyn's leadership.

Every player was encouraged to buy into the team ethic, none more so than two wing forwards Lyn Jones and Mark Perego. Like Ray Gravell before him, Perego ('Rambo' to his friends) was a one-off, more a fitness addict than a rugby fanatic, and though he always wanted to win, he knew there were more important things in life. Fifteen minutes after the final whistle he would appear in a track suit top with a rucksack on his back ready to run back home to Burry Port. On the field his dynamism and total commitment endeared him to the rugby public, whilst his five-minute training schedule, broadcast on BBC's *Scrum V* programme, will remain in our memory for years to come.

Paul Ringer (left), taker of no prisoners, with fellow back-rowers Derek Quinnell and Jeff Squire, protecting no. 9 Terry Holmes from the Romanians at Cardiff in 1979.

(Colorsport)

In the tradition of fine Scarlet flankers, Dafydd Jones targets the opposition midfield, in this case, Chris Mayor of Northampton. Strength and speed around the field coupled with his resilience and stamina made him a formidable opponent.

(Huw Evans Picture Agency)

Rambo on the rumble: Mark Perego tries to escape Robert Howley's clutches. (Huw Evans Picture Agency)

Lyn Jones, a great thinker. (Colorsport)

Alongside him, Lyn Jones was a great thinker, a footballing wing forward who always knew what was happening around him. Time and time again he put others into space, typically floating a perfectly weighted pass to wings Ieuan Evans or Wayne Proctor, who would sprint away for vital tries. Indeed, I think that Lyn Jones could have excelled at scrum half at the top level.

Before making my final choice of wing forwards for the Greatest Scarlets XV Ever, I want to mention another two on my shortlist. Simon Easterby joined the club from Leeds. Irish on his mother's side, English on his father's, he was in a position to choose which country he wanted to represent. Possessing tactical nous, Simon always led from the front and was described by his fellow professionals as a fearless fighter. His stubborn determination to succeed was certainly in evidence when he joined the 2005 British and Irish Lions as a replacement. He was one of few to fire on all cylinders on that tour.

He captained the Scarlets in a vital Heineken Cup encounter against Wasps at Stradey Park when Shaun Edwards in a pre-match interview categorically stated that Simon Easterby had to be stopped if Wasps were to win. They failed! One of the Scarlets' greatest performances in the modern era was against Ulster at a rain-drenched Ravenhill. I was there and it was an awesome display; the Welshmen ran riot in foul weather scoring breathtaking tries in an exhibition of free-flowing total rugby. Simon was the catalyst in a Scarlet rampage. Nor will I forget the sight of the horrific mess on his face as he triumphantly walked off the field at Stade Ernest Wallon where his team had destroyed the might of Toulouse. Simon, no longer with the Scarlets, has recently been appointed forwards coach for his beloved Ireland.

I always knew that Gareth Jenkins would turn out to be a top player. He was a star as a youngster with a strong physical presence and dexterous handling skills. He was strong and athletic but what made him extra special was

A fearless fighter, Simon Easterby wades into the Wasps in 2008.

(Huw Evans Picture Agency)

his attitude – he couldn't bear to lose. I played with Gareth Jenkins for ten seasons and I have no hesitation in saying that at his peak he was as good as any wing forward in Welsh rugby. A knee injury ultimately wrecked his career but time spent as player coach at Furnace RFC was the ideal preparation for his future role as coaching supremo at Llanelli.

A pumped-up Gareth Jenkins fought a running battle with Keith Murdoch in the 1972 All Blacks match. The New Zealand prop took exception to some borderline exchanges and the Llanelli wing forward was continually battered in an attempt to keep him under control. Murdoch was a real hard man but Gareth got up every time a punch was delivered, never taking a backward step and continued his running combat with the moustachioed monster up to the final whistle.

Ultimately, however, I had no hesitation whatsoever in selecting my two wing forwards.

Gareth Jenkins, ball in two hands and with Derek Quinnell on his inside and Selwyn Williams outside, outpaces the Wasps back row in 1976. (PA Images)

Derek Quinnell was an exceptional rugby player who could produce outstanding performances whether it be at no. 8, in the second row or at blind-side wing forward – no mean feat in itself. As I have already chosen R.H. Williams and Delme Thomas to play in the second row and Scott Quinnell at no. 8, it was a formality that Derek would wear the no. 6 shirt.

It was in this position that he played for the Lions against New Zealand in 1971 and it was a decision that caused a great deal of discussion at the time. The press were astounded that such an arch-strategist as Carwyn James could gamble on such an untried combination in the forwards. What they didn't know was that Derek was equally capable at wing forward as at no. 8 and that in the former position he could keep a close eye on the All Black scrum half and danger man, Sid Going. This he did to perfection. The Lions won 13–3 with Derek delivering a man-of-the-match performance. This he continued to do every time he played for the Scarlets, Wales, the Lions and the Barbarians and this is why he was an automatic choice in my back row.

My open-side wing forward had to be Ivor Jones, who first appeared in a scarlet jersey against London Welsh on Boxing Day 1922 and apart from a season representing Birmingham RFC (he ventured to the Midlands when job opportunities were scarce in west Wales) he played 522 games for the club, scoring 1200 points in a career which lasted from 1922 to 1938. According to rugby's journalists at the time, Ivor was the finest forward of the post First World War era and it was indeed a travesty that he was never selected for Wales after his return from New Zealand with the Lions in 1930. Rowe Harding, a fellow pupil of Ivor Jones at Loughor Infants School, described Ivor on the field in *Rugby Reminiscences and Opinions* (The Pilot Press, 1929):

> … lurking around the base of the scrum like a lurcher dog, anticipating and smothering his opponents' tactics, living on the limit of the off-side rule himself, pointing out to the referee any infringements by rival wing forwards, profiting to the full from any penalty exacted, never exerting himself unduly, but on the spot when danger threatened and feeding his own backs with a stream of shrewd passes.

While touring New Zealand with the Lions, Ivor was described in the local press as the best wing forward ever to have played in the islands. It was the red-headed forward's determination coupled with his natural talent which made such an impression. J.B.G. Thomas reminds us in *Fifty-*

The Mighty Quin himself, Derek Quinnell, about to pick up loose ball under pressure from South Africa's Morne du Plessis during the second Lions Test in 1980. Adding moral support are Bill Beaumont (left) and Graham Price.

(Colorsport)

two Famous Tries (Pelham Books, 1966) how Ivor endeared himself to the New Zealand public and achieved immortal fame as a Test player. Only minutes remained at Carisbrook Park, Dunedin on June 21, 1930 when Jones struck:

> It was 3–3 with the British defending desperately in their own 25. Porter put the ball into the scrum and the pass should have reached its target but, no, Ivor Jones with the speed of a bullet snatched the ball out of the air with an amazing interception and he was gone before any New Zealander could say… 'Llanelly'! They gave chase but near the half-way line stood the greatest tackler of his day, George Nepia. Like a cool calm, assured tiger he was ready to strike and kill, and floor the audacious Welshman. Jones, out of the corner of his left eye, saw the young, dapper, elusive Morley, running as if his very life depended upon it. Jones got to Nepia and with uncanny anticipation, delayed his pass until the last possible fraction of a second. As the iron arms of Nepia wrapped around the forward, the ball was fed out to the safe hands of the sprinting Jack Morley. The All Black Cooke, a fast runner himself, was closing rapidly and Morley had another 50 yards to go. Cooke got to his target but Morley got to the line first. The Lions had won the first test match 6-3!

No try! Ivor Jones's try against the 1953 All Blacks at Stradey was disallowed.

In 1969, Ivor returned to New Zealand as President of the Welsh Rugby Union. The respect shown to him was quite unbelievable! He was still remembered as one of the greatest wing forwards to have toured the country. They all wanted to shake his hand. He was a colossus in rugby terms and remains a Scarlet legend to this very day. In 1930, the *New Zealand Free Lance* penned this ditty in his honour:

> Ivor Jones, a six-footer from Wales,
> Is a whale amongst footballing males,
> Though from Wales he's not wailing
> When all's not plain sailing,
> But revels in blazing the trails.

Derek Quinnell and Ivor Jones: two whales amongst footballing males!

'Brilliant by Quinnell!' Derek (right) is about to play his part in the greatest try ever as the Barbarians take on New Zealand at Cardiff in 1973. The eventual try scorer, Gareth Edwards, is some way behind, watching John Dawes passing to Tommy David.

(Colorsport/Colin Elsey)

The Greatest Scarlets XV Ever

14 IEUAN EVANS

15 TERRY DAVIES

11 J.J. WILLIAMS

13 RAY GRAVELL

12 ALBERT JENKINS

10 STEPHEN JONES

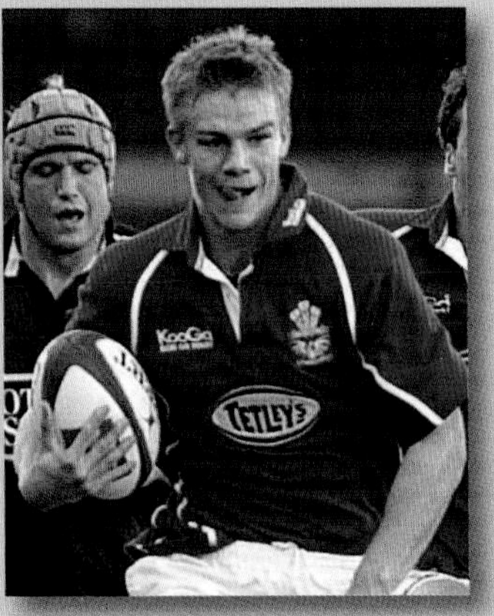

9 DWAYNE PEEL

1 BARRY LLEWELYN

2 NORMAN GALE

3 LAURANCE DELANEY

4 R.H. WILLIAMS

5 DELME THOMAS

6 DEREK QUINNELL

8 SCOTT QUINNELL

7 IVOR JONES

Acknowledgements

I'm indebted to so many people for all their help in the preparation of this book, many of whom have also been supportive of me in so many other areas of my life over the years, not least my wife Pat, of course. Likewise my son Steven and his wife Angharad, our grandchildren Ela and Steffan, and our youngest son, James. Also, because he is always in our thoughts, our lovely little baby son Stewart, whom we lost exactly forty years ago.

I also want to acknowledge the following:

> Llanelli Schoolboys for producing so many outstanding players over the years; my home club, Felinfoel, who guided me through my formative years; committeemen and stalwarts at Stradey Park (1966–1981), including the ladies who produced cordon bleu meals; all those fans at Stradey, the greatest supporters in the world; Willie John McBride for his foreword; the late Mervyn Bowen, the PE teacher who nurtured so many fine rugby players in his time at Coleshill; Llanelli historian Les Williams for unearthing so many facts and figures; friends in the rugby community in Carmarthenshire and all over the world, especially those close friends, upon whom I'm sure to become ever more reliant, now that I'm a senior citizen; Ceri Wyn Jones and all at Gomer, along with the excellent Alun Wyn Bevan for all his enthusiasm, encouragement, prompting and word processing.

I wish the present-day Scarlets all the best and can only hope that they are supported as warmly and faithfully as previous generations of Scarlets were by the club and community. I had occasion to visit an old people's home in Llanelli recently and who should I spot there staring wistfully out of the window but Peter Evans, who captained Llanelli against the 1953 All Blacks. His eyes lighted up when he saw me and he pointed out of the window, drawing my attention to where in the distance Stradey Park had once stood. He was emotional yet dignified as he spoke: 'See that over there, Phil – that was our home; Stradey was our home.'
I sincerely hope that the present-day encumbents of that special Scarlet jersey, and those to come, will always think as fondly of Parc y Scarlets.